"An important and needed update of the rules of community organizing in the Internet Age. But unlike Saul Alinsky's *Rules for Radicals*, there is nothing cynical or manipulative in Eric Liu's vision. We may disagree on many policy specifics, but we agree that dispersed citizen power is the new normal, and that 'many smalls can surpass a few bigs.' This hopeful and essential book shows us how to take responsibility for our democracy."

— Matt Kibbe, founder of Free the People

"Those who want a more sustainable and just future often feel powerless against big corporations and the 1 percent. After reading Eric Liu's book, I see we do have power; we just need to better understand and leverage it. Read this book and let's get to work!"

— Annie Leonard, executive director of Greenpeace USA

"Many of us want to make change but don't know where to start. Liu's wide-ranging career proves he is a doer—and with this thoughtful, forthright, provocative work, he empowers us to be the same."

— Brittany N. Packnett, activist and cofounder of Campaign Zero

"There is no more pressing time than now to understand your own power and use it, and there is no better guide to doing so than Eric Liu. This book is a way of living, individually and collectively, in a changing America."

— Jose Antonio Vargas, founder and CEO of Define American

"*You're More Powerful Than You Think* lays out a clear, practical model for organizing that will be hugely valuable to a new generation of social and political activists—at a moment when the nation badly needs them."

— E. J. Dionne, author of *Why the Right Went Wrong: Conservatism—From Goldwater to Trump and Beyond*

"This is a smart, insightful book about one of the most timely topics of our times: how to create change. With practical examples and keen analysis, Eric Liu offers sure strategies on how you can maximize your power, organize communities, reframe the narrative, and change your world."

— Lynn Povich, author of *The Good Girls Revolt: How the Women of* Newsweek *Sued Their Bosses and Changed the Workplace*

You're More
Powerful
Than You Think

Also by Eric Liu:

*A Chinaman's Chance: One Family's Journey and the
Chinese American Dream*

*The Gardens of Democracy: A New Story of Citizenship, the
Economy, and the Role of Government* (coauthored with
Nick Hanauer)

Imagination First (coauthored with Scott
Noppe-Brandon)

The True Patriot (coauthored with Nick Hanauer)

Guiding Lights: How to Mentor and Find Life's Purpose

The Accidental Asian: Notes of a Native Speaker

NEXT: Young American Writers on the New Generation
(editor)

You're More Powerful Than You Think

A CITIZEN'S GUIDE
to MAKING CHANGE HAPPEN

Eric Liu

PublicAffairs
NEW YORK

Published by PublicAffairs™, an imprint of Perseus Books, LLC, a subsidiary
of Hachette Book Group, Inc.

PublicAffairs books are available at special discounts for bulk purchases in the
U.S. by corporations, institutions, and other organizations. For more information, please contact the Special Markets Department at Perseus Books, 2300
Chestnut Street, Suite 200, Philadelphia, PA 19103, call (800) 810-4145, ext.
5000, or e-mail special.markets@perseusbooks.com.

Book design by Amy Quinn

Library of Congress Cataloging-in-Publication Data

Names: Liu, Eric, author.
Title: You're more powerful than you think : a citizen guide to making change
    happen / Eric Liu.
Description: New York : Public Affairs, [2017]
Identifiers: LCCN 2016049523| ISBN 9781610397070 (hardback) | ISBN
    9781610397087 (ebook)
Subjects: LCSH: Political participation--United States. | Power (Social
    sciences)--United States. | BISAC: POLITICAL SCIENCE / Civics &
    Citizenship. | POLITICAL SCIENCE / Political Process / Political
Advocacy.
Classification: LCC JF799 .L58 2017 | DDC 322.40973--dc23 LC record avail-
    able at https://lccn.loc.gov/2016049523First Edition

10 9 8 7 6 5 4 3 2 1

For Jená

CONTENTS

PROLOGUE
IMMOKALEE AND POTTERSVILLE

Picture a ripe, red tomato. Perhaps there's one in your kitchen. If it's nearby, hold it. Feel its heft. Consider its origins.

There's a fair chance it was picked in Florida, home to a $600-million tomato industry; and if so, a fair chance it was picked in Immokalee, in the sweltering southwest of the state, where much of the industry is concentrated; and if so, a fair chance it was picked by someone who not that many years ago was, in essence, a slave.

Immokalee isn't a place most Americans have seen. But most Americans have eaten the fruits of its vast harvest. And because the picking of tomatoes can't be mechanized, that harvest has always been by hand. By the hands of migrant workers, mainly from Mexico and South America, who were abused physically and verbally and sexually, who were entrapped in debt peonage, paid by the bucket and not the punishing hours in the field, yet whose meager wages were routinely stolen by their overseers, and who were pistol-whipped and chained in locked containers if they complained.

These workers were the very definition of powerlessness. They had no recourse. No advocates. No fluency in the language of their own domination. They were socially dead to the rest of the United States.

And yet, starting in 1993, they came alive. A few of them began to meet secretly in a local church. They resolved, together, to act. First they organized communitywide work stoppages, then hunger strikes, then mass marches hundreds of miles long. They became the Coalition of Immokalee Workers. The press took notice. The workers fought for better pay, and after five years, they finally got a raise from the growers. They fought for such small dignities as shaded rest areas. They earned the currencies that people crave once they achieve subsistence: respect and recognition. They were *seen*.

And they didn't stop there. Once they escaped invisibility, they were determined to undo the bigger system of involuntary servitude. They worked with prosecutors to build cases against their traffickers and captors. Those investigations and convictions freed over 1,200 farmworkers from captivity and forced labor.

They didn't stop there, either. They realized that the machinery of their exploitation was powered by supermarket and fast-food chains that buy produce in mass quantities and create pressure to drive costs down. So in 2001, they organized the first-ever farmworker boycott of a fast-food company, against Taco Bell; four years later Taco Bell's parent company agreed to raise wages and reform its supply chain. With this victory came more allies, more assistance from more experts of all kinds.

And they didn't stop there. They pressured McDonald's and Burger King to agree to the same terms. They organized the Fair Food Program, through which these restaurant and retail chains would buy only from growers who paid a fair wage and abided by a code of conduct stricter than federal law. The buyers agreed to contribute some of the same pittance they once squeezed from the workers—a penny per bucket—to a common fund for worker health, safety, and education. Wal-Mart, with its market-moving scale, joined in 2014. Over $10 million has been paid into the fund in its first seasons. The pickers of Immokalee fought for a fair chance, and they're still fighting.

So if you sometimes wonder whether you have enough clout to make change happen—how *you* could ever be seen or heard, or have your demands answered—then just think of them. If people who started where *they* started could learn power and transform their lives together, can't anyone? If *they* did it, shouldn't *everyone*?

Now think about where *you* work and live and ask yourself: Who runs this place?

It's not that simple a question. There are certain public offices you can identify: mayor or city manager, council members or commissioners. Widen the lens. What businesses dominate the local economy? Who in those businesses has a real say in the town's affairs? Now wider still. Where are the arenas where deals are made, and to whom are they open? Who are the fixers and the enforcers? Are there groups or blocs or interests that always seem to get their way? Who *really* runs this place?

Once you have a sense of an answer, ask another question: How could it be different?

This brings us to what I call the Pottersville flip. In Frank Capra's classic film *It's a Wonderful Life*, George Bailey gets to see what life would be like if he'd never been born. In this counterfactual world, his hometown of Bedford Falls—an idyll of trust and mutual aid and democratic pride—becomes Pottersville, a race-to-the-bottom grid of slums, trashy bars, and pawnshops all owned by the richest man in town, Mr. Potter.

Many American towns in the three generations since *It's a Wonderful Life* have become a lot more like Pottersville than Bedford Falls, in the sense that wealth and clout have consolidated into the hands of one or a few. But wherever your town might fall on the Bedford Falls–to–Pottersville spectrum, imagine flipping places.

Imagine, if you live in a place where you and your neighbors have been crushed by the unseen force of someone else's wealth and wants, what it would be like to be Bedford Falls. Or imagine, if you live in a place where civic health is high and opportunity abounds, what it would be like to descend into Pottersville.

Now run the same thought experiment for the other places in your life: Who runs this company? This campus? This state? Who, if you want to change custom or culture or policy, do you have to see, win over, pressure, shame, praise, or *be* to get the change you want? Who runs this neighborhood, this party, this club or association? Who decides who gets what? What counts as a fair chance?

To ask the question is to begin to change the answer.

The immigrant pickers of Immokalee may never have seen or even heard of *It's a Wonderful Life*. George Bailey is probably not part of their cultural vocabulary. But they've definitely done the

Pottersville flip. They imagined the opposite of helplessness and the inverse of invisibility. They seeded the change they needed. They are harvesting it now.

Go back to that ripe, red tomato, whether in your mind's eye or on your kitchen counter. Appreciate the world of possibility within it. And let it be a humble reminder to you:

You're more powerful than you think.

PART I

THE AGE OF CITIZEN POWER

OUR MOMENT, OUR POWER, OUR PLAN

OUR MOMENT

Here is what people have been doing the last few years:

The Arab Spring, the Orange Revolution, the Maidan protests, the Green Revolution, the Cedar Revolution, the *indignados*, the Umbrella Revolution, the Brexit, anti-government protests in Iceland, Poland, South Korea, Ethiopia, Hungary, Thailand, Brazil. In the United States, we've had Occupy Wall Street, the Tea Party, the Dreamers, Black Lives Matter, $15 Now, Standing Rock, Feel the Bern, and then, of course, the Trump Train.

Not every one of these movements has, in a conventional sense, "succeeded." In fact, most have not (yet). But they're all connected. And they're still coming. Occupy begat We Are the 99%

begat Fast Food Forward begat $15 Now begat the Bernie Sanders campaign. The Tea Party harnessed a radical anti-establishment spirit that seized and then consumed the Republican Party, fueled Donald Trump's election, unleashed a new populism, and created a "none-of-the-above" opening for libertarians.

This is a moment of citizen power. And that is nowhere more visible than in the turbulence of American political and civic life.

The coming-out of undocumented immigrants; the gradual then sudden triumph of marriage equality activists; the counteroffensive for religious liberty; demonstrations against racial inequity; demonstrations for free speech; the rising voices of sexual assault survivors; the emergence of moms for gun responsibility; the unadorned anger of nativists and white nationalists; the rise of Native American environmental activism; the obliteration of elite gatekeepers in party politics, consumer markets, mass media, pop culture—all are evidence of the same bewildering reality.

The old deal is dead. There is no new deal yet.

Citizens today no longer have to accept the bundles—the one-size-fits-all packages—that the monopolies of politics and business have long forced upon us. Unbundling is everywhere, from how we get the news to how we listen to music or watch television to how we catch a ride across town to how we label ourselves by party, gender, or race.

There is an upbeat, utopian version of this story that's all about an explosion of individual choice. But of course the unbundling is happening *to* us as well, in ways that have eaten away at our cohesion, security, and dignity. Social contracts—of trust and common cause—have been unbundled by technologies that sift and sort us ever more narrowly. Collective economic arrangements—pensions, benefits, livable wages, worker safety—have been unbundled by the Uberization and globalization of work.

As a result, in greater and growing numbers, we Americans no longer feel in control of our own everyday lives. We have little say in a workplace that makes us expendable. Our lives as consumers are dominated by distant, impersonal brands. In our lives as citizens too many of us are passive spectators or the clients of distant bureaucracies. We have a surplus of stuff and a deficit of attention and purpose. As we retreat to smaller circles of kith and kin, the commons goes to seed.

All this is propelled by a relentlessly upward concentration of wealth. Since 1980, the share of national income flowing to the wealthiest 1 percent has tripled. Since the end of the Great Recession in 2010, over 90 percent of the recovery's gains have gone to the 1 percent. Median wages have barely moved in forty years, while CEO pay has increased tenfold. More than half the benefits of federal tax breaks flow to the wealthiest 5 percent, while low-income families get nearly nothing. Today the greatest determinant of whether an American child will end up poor or rich is whether parents are poor or rich. By the standards of our national self-story, that is profoundly un-American.

Meanwhile, economic concentration of power begets *political* concentration of power. Congress today is now driven by the policy preferences of wealthy individuals and corporations. A comprehensive study of congressional action by the political scientists Benjamin Page and Martin Gilens showed that when the average American's policy views clash with those of the rich, the rich almost always prevail. The average American is heard only if wealthy donors happen to be saying the same thing. Congress, redistricted to make itself challenger-proof, is walled off against reform. Meanwhile, Republicans use trumped-up charges of election fraud to keep low-income voters of color from voting. And government insiders from both parties cycle through a perpetual revolving door to Wall Street.

But we knew all this already: the system truly has been rigged.

What's new is that this unprecedented concentration of power is now giving rise to a Great Push Back: a sprawling, disorderly effort by citizens of the right, the left, and the scrambled everywhere-else—people of every color and faith—to challenge monopolized power in all its forms and to demand a greater say in how things are run. The revolutions promised by both Sanders and Trump are still coalescing, even if only one of them has the power of the federal government behind him.

And this Great Push Back—this chaotic, contagious cross-ideological revolt of the smalls—is not the end of the story. It's just the raucous beginning. (Also, there is no end.)

It's made all the more turbulent by another great shift underway: the delinking of whiteness and Americanness. The imminent arrival of an America that is majority-of-color—even as the power structure has remained predominantly white, and even as uneducated whites face declining opportunities and life expectancies—has amplified the anxiety and expectation and volatility already in the air. It has made populists out of racists, and vice versa. It has emboldened social justice advocates and white supremacists alike to press their claims more impatiently.

At some point we may reach a stable new equilibrium in political life. Before then, we can expect many more kinds of confrontation between the people in charge and The People. Between monopoly and its discontents. "Power," as Frederick Douglass said, "concedes nothing without a demand."

But here's the thing: there is a gap between making demands and making them happen. It is the gap between the rhetoric of revolution and the actual changes in values, systems, habits, and skills that adds up to a revolution.

This book is designed to help close this "revolution gap": to help you make better demands—and then to make them a reality. It will give you new ways of understanding power in civic life and new tools for claiming and exercising it.

OUR POWER

Let's start with a simple definition: power is the capacity to ensure that others do as you would want them to do.

If that sounds menacing or distasteful, or makes you feel squeamish, I understand. And I invite you to get over it.

Power is something we are often uncomfortable naming and talking about explicitly. In the culture and mythology of democracy, power is supposed to reside with the people. End of story. Further inquiry unnecessary and unwelcome. In our everyday talk, power has a negative moral vibe. *Power-mad. Power-hungry. Power grab. Power trip.* It's a dirty word. Which is why we so often soften it with such euphemisms as "voice" or "strength."

But power is no more inherently good or evil than fire or physics. It just is. The only question is whether we will try to understand and harness it.

If power is the capacity to ensure that others do as you would want them to do, *civic power* is that capacity exercised by citizens in public, whether in elections or government or in social and economic arenas.

I say "ensure" rather than "compel" or "make," because power is as often about persuasion or contagion as coercion. And when I say "citizens" here, I do not mean only people with the right papers; I mean all members of the body politic, who can and do contribute to our common life, whatever their documentation status.

Power in civic life takes many forms: force, wealth, state action, ideas, social norms, numbers. And it flows through many conduits: institutions, organizations, networks, laws and rules, narratives and ideologies. Map these forms and conduits against each other and you get what we think of as "the power structure."

But the problem today is that too many people aren't able to draw, read, or follow such a map. Too many people are profoundly—and willfully—illiterate in power: what it is, what forms it takes, who has it, who doesn't, why that is, how it is exercised.

As a result, it's become ever easier for those who *do* understand how power operates in civic life—those who understand how a bill becomes a law, yes, but also how a friendship becomes a subsidy or how a bias becomes a policy or how a slogan becomes a movement—those folks are more capable than ever of wielding disproportionate influence and filling the void created by the ignorance of the majority.

How does a friendship become a subsidy? Seamlessly, when senior government staffers become corporate lobbyists and work their relationships to benefit their new masters. How does a bias become a policy? Insidiously, as with stop-and-frisk. How does a slogan become a movement? Virally, as when Tea Party activists co-opt "Don't Tread on Me," or Black Lives Matter turns a hashtag into a movement.

But most people don't see or care to look for these realities. Much of this ignorance, this power illiteracy, is intentional. And that compounds the problem.

There are some young people who think the whole business is sordid and would rather do community service or direct action and exempt themselves from politics altogether.

There are some techies who think that the cure-all for power imbalances or abuses is simply more data and transparency, and that tech networks are *inherently* beneficial.

There are some on the left who think only business has power and some on the right who think only government has power; both blinded by their selective outrage.

There are the naïve who believe that good things just happen, and the cynical who believe that bad things just happen: the fortunate and unfortunate alike who believe their lot is simply what happens to them, rather than the alterable result of a prior arrangement, an inherited allocation, of *power*.

But as the sociologist C. Wright Mills wrote in *The Power Elite*: "To accept either view—of all history as conspiracy or all of history as drift—is to relax the effort to understand the facts of power and the ways of the powerful."

As a result of this creeping public fatalism, we now have depressingly low levels of civic participation, knowledge, engagement, and awareness. Political life has been subcontracted out to a band of professionals—money people, message people, outreach people. The rest of us are made to feel like amateurs, as in *suckers*. We become demotivated to learn more about how things work. And this pervasive power illiteracy becomes, in a vicious cycle, both a cause and a consequence of the concentration of opportunity, wealth, and clout in society.

This is why reimagining civics as the teaching and learning of *power* is so necessary—now perhaps more than at any time in the last century. If you don't learn how to practice power, someone else will do it for you—in your name, on your turf, with your voice, and often against your interests.

Power plays out in every arena of life, from the home to the workplace to the public square. In this book our focus is on power in political and civic life—how we live in public. And the core question of such power is this: Who decides?

Every aspect of collective existence in a complex society is the result of countless layers of countless decisions, including decisions not to challenge long-ago decisions.

Think: How did the railroad tracks get put down in my town and who decided what would be the wrong side and the right side of those tracks? Why does one employer get tax breaks and subsidies but not another? Why is this community center getting funded instead of that one? Why a new jail instead of preschool? Who decided that?

When a city passes an anti-discrimination ordinance to protect gay, lesbian, and transgender people, but then the state preempts the ordinance, what unfolds is an argument not only about local government law but also about culture and identity. When a national political party has a system for allocating delegates, and one candidate's campaign comes to resent that system, the conflict may unfold in the language of parliamentary rules but it is, more deeply, a matter of muscle and "street heat."

Who decides? All politics turns on that question. The answer is in furious flux today. If you are illiterate in power, if you cannot speak the language of who has clout and how it is exercised, you will not even realize you've been excluded from the question.

OUR PLAN

Before we go through the plan for the pages to come, I want to make one thing clear. This book is not about personal empowerment in the self-help sense. There is no chicken soup for anyone's soul here. Nor is it about empowerment in the Machiavellian sense. You'll find nothing in these pages about how to manipulate the boss or edge out workplace rivals. I offer not the courtier's view of power but the *citizen's* view.

The citizen's view is by definition greater than the self because the citizen—a member of the body, a contributor to community—is by definition acting in a social context. To be sure, the citizen's view of power is not selfless. It is often quite selfish. But whereas self-help and self-advancement focus on the individual, often in isolation, citizen power is about identity and action in the collective: how *we* make change happen *together*.

Something else to be up front about: This book is for underdogs and challengers, not top dogs and incumbents. It's for people who want to be change agents, not defenders of the status quo. That change can emanate from the left or from the right. In many cases, it will scramble the lines *between* left and right. But in all cases, this book is about democratizing power rather than hoarding it.

As the coming pages will demonstrate, hoarding is not just morally repugnant; it is systemically suicidal. If we want our society to work for everyone, it is imperative that we learn to circulate power and literacy in power far more widely.

And literacy isn't just a metaphor. Imagine finding yourself in a foreign land. If you can't read or write the language, life is very challenging. Street signs, storefronts, newspapers, public notices: all are undecipherable to you. Because you don't know what you don't know, you become an easy mark for fraud, you waste energy and time on everyday tasks, you are cut out of chances to improve your situation, you are in every sense voiceless. You might survive, but you will never thrive.

Not knowing how to read or write *power* has exactly the same effects. Power is a language. It has a grammar and a syntax. It expresses our wants and needs, and is the medium by which those wants and needs are negotiated and addressed. Ignorance of that language is harmful to your aspirations and to your well-being.

So literacy in power means understanding the what, the how, and the why of power. That's the plan for the rest of this book. In Part II, we will focus on *what* power truly is and how to imagine it anew. We will explore three core laws of power that shape the patterns of public life—and that challenge us not to give away our power carelessly but to circulate it wisely.

Then in Part III, we will examine *how* to practice power—and specifically, how those laws demand three kinds of strategies for the citizen who wants to create change. Finally, Part IV examines *why* you'd want civic power. To what ends are you learning about the elements and the strategies of political action? What are the moral purposes and ethical foundations of your desire for clout?

In every part, we will look at cases from the past and present. Full disclosure: most are from the contemporary United States. That's not jingoism or parochialism. It's knowing what I know best. And it's trusting that you'll be able and willing to connect dots across place and time to your own situation.

We will also look at cases from across the ideological spectrum. You may not like the positions or beliefs of some of the people you will meet. But a skillful citizen finds lessons everywhere. This is important. In case you couldn't tell, I am not the mythical creature called the Impartial Observer. I write as a citizen who has progressive and communitarian views and who has put those views into practice—in government and policy making, in concerted citizen action, and in the publication of ideas.

But I also write as the founder of a cross-ideological organization, Citizen University, that brings together people from the Occupy left, the Tea Party right, and many points between. We challenge each other to find common interests. We generate unlikely collaborations and friendships. We engage where we can in mutual aid because although we will often disagree on policy and intellectual paradigms, we can all agree that this is a time to take on entrenched monopolists—and to boost citizen power.

The analogy I often use in my work, because I am a baseball fanatic, is this: I grew up in upstate New York and I'm a Yankees fan. I hate the Boston Red Sox. But I share with Red Sox fans an abiding interest *in the underlying health of the game*. The more people who know how to play, and the more resources there are for people to learn how to play, and the less corrupt and rigged the game is, and the less rigid a wall there is between amateurs and professionals, the better it is for everyone. Let's first make sure, together, that the game is not sick—that it prospers in every way. *Then* my Yanks can go beat the Sox.

The underlying health of civic life today is poor. The Trump presidency was born of decades of democratic decline. The clubs and associations where people used to practice citizenship are moribund. Everyday journalism that holds local power to account is evaporating. Muckraking investigative journalism is even rarer. Civic education in the schools is disappearing, and where it survives, it is often reduced to a bland "lowest-controversy denominator" that makes civics unsexy—or worse, it's hijacked by history-blind fanatics who call Moses one of the Founding Fathers or describe enslaved people as "workers." The game is sick. And it's not a game.

Let's begin the work of healing it.

PART II

HOW TO UNDERSTAND POWER

POWER IS A GIFT

Why do most people think power is a dirty word? Because they think it means coercion and violence. They associate it with the worst in human nature. And there's no question that power can involve all those forms of domination, and more. Lord Acton's dictum—that power corrupts, and absolute power corrupts absolutely—is the world's most famous statement on power because it accords with our deep intuitions.

But I want to propose a different way of seeing power. In fact, I want to propose a different way of *seeing*. Though it may not seem as intuitive as Acton's dictum, what I offer is perhaps more true than intuition, in the way that facts of nature like heat or light or weight are true well before we sense them—indeed, whether we ever sense them at all.

How we see is shaped partly by language, especially the metaphors we use. For example, I have said that power is like fire: inherently neither good nor evil, but deployable for both and thus a phenomenon to understand and master. That metaphor treats power as a tool. It suggests that power doesn't corrupt character so much as it reveals it: *What will you do with this flame?*

Here is another metaphor: power is like water. It flows all around us at all times. Sometimes it takes the liquid form of politics-in-action, a turbulent flow with crosscurrents and strong undertows. Sometimes it takes the solid form of settled law: policy is power frozen. Sometimes it is like vapor in the air, invisibly shaping the climate and our behavior in just the way beliefs or ideology or emotions do.

But how we see is not just a matter of language. It is also a matter of moral imagination. Whether you conceptualize power as fire, water, mass, force, or something else altogether, the deepest truth is that we the people are not merely the passive receptacles or objects of power. We are the very source of power. We do not just receive power as it passes through us or acts upon us. We generate it. We give it.

What I am saying is that power is a gift.

This is the most basic reason that you're more powerful than you think. And it is a notion that, to some, sounds terribly naïve or wrongheaded. So let me explain.

Power is a gift in several senses. First, it is something that emanates from us, that inheres in us. There is a religious way to put this, and many thoughtful believers would describe the life force that God puts in each of us—a force that enables us to exist, and then to make and repair the world—as a sacred gift. This is the power to create, and as the theologian Andy Crouch has written so eloquently, it has not the imperative spirit of "Make it so" but the invitational spirit of "Let there be." The power of genesis is not to oppress but to actualize: to spark flourishing.

I happen not to have been raised in any faith tradition. But in my own secular-spiritual American brand of *civic* religion—based on the texts and acts of our founding creed—I believe that human dignity requires freedom and the power to make of oneself and one's world all that one can. Such power is a gift, a human birthright. Citizenship of the United States, for those of us with the dumb luck to have been born into it, wraps that universal gift in a particular form of privilege—unearned at birth, perhaps, but redeemable by a lifetime of deeds and *contributions*.

Second, power is a gift in the sense of a talent—and more than that, an obligation to pass the talent on. When we say someone is a gifted painter or singer or runner or healer, we mean she has been given something special and precious. We also imply she has a responsibility to cultivate and to share that something special with the world. She has been endowed not only with inalienable rights but also inalienable duties.

A kind of circulation is at work here, and it is perpetual. Lewis Hyde, in his classic book *The Gift*, describes the making of true art as an endless cycle of gift exchange and warns about the dangers of treating art and creativity as commodities. A commodity mindset deadens human bonds of trust and affection. In Hyde's view, talent is not primarily a product for the market. It is first a gift for humanity. And the same holds for power. True power, which recycles endlessly, demands that those who hold it, ever so briefly, must do so for others.

The third, most literal, and most important way that power is a gift is simply that we give it. I cannot underscore that enough. *We give it.* Every person and institution with power in our society today has it because we give it to them. I know it does not feel that way. Most of us don't remember actively giving power to those people and institutions. But we did. We do.

Whether you live in a democracy that's become sclerotic and corrupt, like ours, or an authoritarian society that wants to control what you do and learn, it is important to remember that others don't take our power so much as we give it away. We give it away by not organizing or participating, out of a fatalistic sense that it doesn't matter, that "my vote won't count anyway." But mark well: there is no such thing as not voting. Not voting *is* voting—to hand power to others, whose interests may be inimical to your own. And not organizing *is* organizing—for the people who mean to dominate you.

Consider every form of power I listed earlier: force, wealth, state action, ideas, social norms, numbers. Every one originates from us. From you. That doesn't mean you can make yourself a millionaire by wishing it so. It does mean that money, which takes the form of a symbol, is an agreement between you, me, and the world to have that symbol mean something. If you refuse agreement, if you no longer honor promises made in that symbol, you are rediscovering your power. That is true whether you are an individual or a sovereign state.

Consider Donald Trump. This man gained power because—and only because—we gave it to him. We gave him our attention, our hope, our belief, our outrage, our fear, our anxiety. Many gave him their own unused, never-activated potential as change agents. We together gave him a vast voice and an omnipresent face because we lent him our many ears and our many eyes.

Trump "took" power, yes, in the sense that he initiated the exchange and invited it. He provoked us to yield power. But make no mistake: we made him possible. And it's not just Trump. The same dynamic unfolded for Barack Obama in 2008. Candidate Obama had tried to remind us that "We are the change we've been waiting for." But *we* did not have the courage of *his* convictions. We gave him our power, we invested our agency in him, and then many were disappointed when as president he alone could not deliver all that had been hoped for.

That we give power to make the powerful is of course a truth of human relations, not just of presidential politics. It is true with our peers and colleagues, with our friends and relatives. And it is true in everyday civic life, from the neighborhood level up. No one can wield power except as others *yield* power. The power that anyone holds over us originates with us—and can ultimately be reclaimed or redirected by us.

To be clear, this is not "blaming the victim." It does not mean that people who are dominated and demeaned and seemingly stuck in unjust situations somehow asked for it or deserve it. Actually, quite the opposite. It means the victim is not helpless—is, in fact, a source of help.

If the tomato pickers of Immokalee teach us anything, it is that even what looks like a near-total power imbalance is never in fact as severe as it appears. Once those pickers began to help one another, they saw their power compound and grow. From there they found outside help. From there they flipped their fates. Power, they proved, is not only something done *to* us. Power is something done *by* us.

Of course, the "us" in question is an ever-shifting, ever-fragmenting, ever-agglomerating thing. That's politics. That's human interaction in a diverse ecosystem of conflicting desires, needs, and interests. And seeing this ecosystem properly helps us see our own role within it.

It's impossible to imagine the self in isolation. The self exists in social context. Which means that we are constantly generating feedback loops: my response to your response to my response to your action, always cycling around and around. Sometimes we are creating vicious cycles of mistrust and recrimination; sometimes, virtuous cycles of trust and affinity. In politics we move in halls of mirrors, always responding to each other's images at second and third hand.

The investor George Soros calls this dynamic "reflexivity." It's a reality of the stock market, in which booms and busts arise unpredictably and irrationally from countless individual choices because everyone is always responding to everyone's responses to everyone's responses. In the stock market, though, there are definable assets being exchanged at values that can generally be quantified and standardized.

In the arena of civic power, much of what's being traded is unstated and undefined. That makes it much harder to understand. Yet the same patterns emerge as in the market. Patterns of compounding, in which small initial advantages bloom into bigger ones. Patterns of infinite mirroring that quickly distort our perceptions of each other. Patterns of give-and-take that lead people to act with mindsets—self-fulfilling mindsets—of either scarcity or abundance.

These patterns define our lives, yet much of the time we are not conscious of them. We forget to notice the complex interdependence of the world. We seek out conceptual shortcuts and we start to mistake surfaces for the depths. We pretend in America, for instance, that we are rugged individuals. And over time this makes us feel less and less powerful. Why? Because in the end (as in the beginning), there is no such thing as a self-made man or woman. And the pretense is tiring and dispiriting.

But if we see power as a gift, a gift in every sense—as an endowment to nurture, a talent to share, a resource to exchange—then we remember that as a moral matter and as a matter of fact, we are always bound up in webs of relationship, exchange, and obligation. And this is not confining. It is *liberating*. These are what the psychologist C. Terry Warner calls the "bonds that make us free." Relationships and obligations, by reminding us that our responses to the world are contagious, reacquaint us with our own power to create contagion.

Earlier, I defined power as the capacity to ensure that others do as you would like them to do. In the context of a Hobbesian every-man-for-himself image of society, that definition seemed bleak and brutish. But reexamine it now in the light of a gift, in the context of a society that exists only because people tacitly and sometimes expressly have been living a life of mutual aid.

In her book *A Paradise Built in Hell*, Rebecca Solnit describes the unexpected communities that arise spontaneously out of disasters, from the great San Francisco fire of 1906 to Hurricane Katrina in 2005. She refuses to concede that these beautiful communities of displaced strangers helping each other, these rubble-bound utopias, are the exceptions that prove the rule of selfish human nature. She persuasively reframes them, instead, as the condition we naturally yearn for—a paradise we have lost because we fell into a conception of power as domination.

When we see power as a gift, we realize we are perpetually in the position to choose when and whether we will give and to whom—and whether to throw it away or invest it. We perceive anew our own capacity to shape how others respond to us, and thus our capacity to shape the world. We recall that this capacity is ours as humans and citizens, even if circumstances have labeled us second-class humans or citizens. We see that we can remake those circumstances if we share and activate our gift wisely.

This is not naïveté. It is how every movement of social and political reform in our country—indeed, in the world—has ever come to fruition.

In Part III, we will explore many such movements and many strategies for activating the gift of power. But before we do that, it's important to understand the basic dynamics of power itself. In particular, there are three core laws of power that I want to describe. They emerge from the turbulent give-and-take of civic life. They shape how we respond to our situation. And they are central to the work of creating change.

THE THREE LAWS
OF POWER

Let me acknowledge here: it's always risky to assert there are X number of laws about anything. One author has written a book with forty-eight laws of power. In an earlier draft of this book I had a dozen. There is no magic number. And that's fine. This book is meant to be an argument about how power works in civic life and a guide for exercising it. It is *not* meant to be a catalog or encyclopedia of all theoretical aspects of power.

But my argument—that we are in an age of citizen power; that greater fluency in power is both possible and necessary; and fundamentally, that you are more powerful than you think—leads me to focus on a few great patterns I've encountered in my work and in our history. Those patterns recur with enough force and regularity that I'll call them laws.

Here they are:

- First, power *concentrates*. That is, it feeds on itself and compounds (as does powerlessness).
- Second, power *justifies itself*. People invent stories to legitimize the power they have (or lack).
- Third, power is *infinite*. There is no inherent limit on the amount of power people can create.

Together, these three laws create a cycle of monopoly and monopoly busting—a power cycle that is at the very heart of politics and political history. Laws 1 and 2 mean that all societies, left to themselves, gravitate toward a state of hoarded, monopolized, dramatically unequal power. But Law 3 tells us power is not zero-sum. New power can be created from thin air. Which means you can always bypass, displace, or upend a prior state of monopoly.

Law 3 can save us from Laws 1 and 2—if we remember it, and know what to do with it. That's how the cycle turns, when it does. But the tendency in civic life is to get stuck after Law 2 kicks in, which allows incumbent holders of power to perpetuate and extend their dominance.

It's important again to underscore in all three laws the underlying reality that power is a gift. We give it. We nourish these cycles. We yield our own inherent power and direct it to others. The question is whether we become aware enough of that to decide when and whether to *redirect* our power.

To see all this more clearly, let's consider each law in more depth.

LAW 1: POWER CONCENTRATES

What's the best way to get rich? Start rich.

That's not a cynical take on the 1 percent. Or at least not *only* that. It's a statement of social fact. Even when the rules are entirely neutral, in complex systems advantages compound. Left to itself, a market economy will eventually put a massive share of total wealth into a very small number of hands. Of course, what makes it worse is that the rules are never entirely neutral. They are usually skewed by the privileged for the privileged, which only accelerates the compounding.

And what is true of advantage is true of disadvantage. It too compounds. Being poor is expensive. Living and dying poor eats up a far greater share of your income than living and dying rich. Predatory payday loans, the unavailability of affordable housing, the cost of eviction and relocation, the high price of transportation, the regressivity of bank fees and parking tickets and sales taxes, the disproportionate earnings hole that gets created by illness or accident, which of course become more likely when you're tired or underfed—all these features of everyday life for poor Americans exert a strong gravitational pull, making it less likely they can ever achieve "escape velocity" into economic security.

Is this just a feature of the uniquely skewed system of twenty-first-century American life? No. It may be worse here than in other, more fair societies. But the nature of *nature* is to create concentrated clusters. What starts out as a random distribution always ends up in clumps: certain trees get more of the light initially, which enables them to get even more of the light from then on and to grow taller, while other trees become stunted in the shade or simply die.

Scientists who study networks and complex systems call this "path dependence" and "emergence." Small initial variations are amplified by positive feedback loops, sending energy ("buzz," "heat") to certain paths of evolution but not others. Nodes in a network that attract more links early on, even if randomly (that is, independent of whether they "deserved" the early edge), emerge over time as the dominant nodes and drive the evolution of the system as a whole. This is how VHS beat Betamax, how Facebook beat Friendster, how Silicon Valley beat any other region.

In our lives as social beings, we make monopoly. Acting in path-dependent ways, we often unwittingly contribute to concentration of opportunity, attention, and power. We get on bandwagons. We are susceptible to contagions of fame or desirability. The same few experts get quoted in the media, the same investors get insider tips in the stock market, the same celebrities get thought of for prime roles.

The sociologist Robert Merton called this pattern "the Matthew effect," after the passage in scripture describing how privilege and privation both compound ruthlessly: "For unto every one that hath shall be given, and he shall have abundance: but from him that hath not shall be taken even that which he hath."

Our politics over the last forty years has used state action to mechanize the Matthew effect. Trickle-down economic policies, giving preferential treatment to the already wealthy and cutting investments in the poor and middle-income, generated economic inequality. This, in turn, generated more political inequality. Most campaign contributions now come from a rich, tiny sliver of the population. Most lobbying is done on their behalf. So the rich don't only get richer; they get louder. Their voices are heard more than anyone else's. Each form of inequality reinforces the other.

You can extrapolate from there. In the board game Monopoly, eventually someone has everything and everyone else has nothing and the game ends. But in real life, "game over" means catastrophic system collapse for all—including, by the way, the "winner."

In their book *Why Nations Fail*, the economists Daron Acemoglu and James Robinson surveyed societies across continents and eons and found a common pattern. Some, like the ancient Mayans or the slaveholding American South, were designed for extraction. That is, the rulers set things up to suck the maximum amount of wealth and work out of everyone else. Others, like modern Scandinavian nations, were designed for inclusion. That is, things were set up for ever more people to participate ever more actively in commerce, culture, and civic life.

Guess which kind survives?

Though extractive societies often generate great individual fortunes for the people in charge, they are exceedingly brittle. Enslavers always imagine a slave revolt around the corner. Authoritarian states always sense subversion in the unsupervised communications of citizens. Screwing over everyone is exhausting, and a terrible use of everyone's talent. Such societies never get the full benefit of the full potential of the full populace. Worse, such societies have low resilience in a crisis and little ability to adapt to change. Hoarding kills. Eventually it kills even the hoarders.

Which is why, from the Inca Empire to the Soviet Union, extractive societies have been prone to collapse. Power naturally flows to the top. We've established that. But where power flows to the top and *stays there*, without correction or recirculation, a society is likely to die a catastrophic death.

So given this, how is it that extractive regimes with monopolized power—and now, I am referring not only to the Incas or the Soviets but also, increasingly, to *us*—manage to endure as long as they do? The second law helps explain that.

LAW 2: POWER JUSTIFIES ITSELF

The powerful tell tales about why they deserve their status, so that they can feel better about it. So do the powerless. Together, these two sets of stories form an unseen edifice, a prison of the imagination that shrinks *everyone's* scope of possibility about alternative arrangements and allocations of power.

This is an insight as old as storytelling and political community. It's now reinforced by some fascinating research in experimental social science.

What these studies show, in the aggregate, is that with greater relative power comes greater sociopathy: more self-centeredness, increased sensitivity to affront, a sense of entitlement, a belief that high status is not just deserved but natural, deep ignorance about people with less power, a lack of inhibition and respect for social norms.

Donald Trump is the contemptible, cartoonish epitome of this pattern of behavior. But each of us experiences such people every day. Indeed, each of us likely behaves this way more often than we admit. So it isn't necessarily surprising that the powerful have a strong instinct for self-justification. They need to defend their privilege, which is bound up with their identity, and they do so in ways both conscious and unconscious.

What *is* surprising is how often the powerless join them in defending it.

People with low power, these studies indicate, are significantly more trusting than people with high power. Specifically, they are trusting of the people with *high* power. Chalk it up to wishful thinking or what psychologists call "motivated cognition," but when experimental subjects are placed in low-power situations, they very much want to believe that their high-power counterparts are benevolent and worthy of trust. This hopefulness—not based on any particular evidence—arises mainly out of a desire to evade the discomfort of being at the mercy of the more powerful.

Moreover, the powerless must develop sophisticated understandings of the powerful in order to get by. They have to work hard to get in the heads of those who determine what opportunities and outcomes they can enjoy. (The powerful, meanwhile, don't particularly attend to the lives or minds of the powerless because they assume they don't have to.) Consider, for example, how much better enslaved people in the South understood the ways of their white enslavers than vice versa.

But it's not only that those at the bottom must spend a lot of interpretive energy trying to make sense of those above them in the social hierarchy, or that these low-power citizens are primed to assume the best of their "betters," even when it's undeserved. There's one more turn of the screw—by the hand of the powerless.

Psychologists call it "system justification theory," and it posits that people without power tend to blame themselves for their weak situation; worse, they often actively defend the system that renders them powerless. Why? Because it sometimes can be more bearable to make excuses for the system and its inequities than to admit the possibility that you are truly without agency. The latter is a greater threat to your dignity.

Underlying all these dynamics is the presence of cognitive dissonance—the tension between the image we want to have of ourselves and our actual circumstances. Humans always resolve cognitive dissonance in ways that reduce pain. That means explaining away—rationalizing—the embarrassment of being at the bottom. It means buying into legitimizing myths, the cultural narratives and ideologies that explain why the haves have and the have-nots have not.

In the words of one study, by Rob Willer of Stanford University and several other scholars, "The more participants reported feeling powerless, the more they believed that economic inequality was fair and legitimate." That is stunning.

In America we have been told for decades that the wealthy got that way because they earned it through superior smarts and better choices. The powerful earned it by their superior savvy and skill. If only the rest of us had made the right choices with that level of savvy, we too could be enjoying a life of privilege. But we didn't. So for now, we should defer to those at the top and not overtax them (in any sense), and we should trust that the process is fair and their wealth will eventually trickle down to everyone.

This storyline is part of a larger ideology of rugged individualism and free-trade capitalism. And to be clear: the wealthy and powerful made it up. But why did the rest of us *accept* it? Because it at least implied that improvement was possible with greater grit and wiser effort. It implied that in a market driven by merit, we too could be winners one day. The alternative—that we are but pawns and cannon fodder, stuck no matter how hard we try, in control of very little of our own fate—was too hard to face. Self-blame became a form of self-justification and coping: *It's not you, America; it's me.*

Until now. What has made a moment like ours so tumultuous and exciting and dangerous is that trickle-down legitimizing myths have lost their grip. People without power—or who feel in relative terms that they've lost power—have decided to reject elite rationalizations of the status quo. Trump supporters and Sanders supporters may not have shared a political style or a moral palette, but they did share in spades this readiness to "burn it all down."

People will tell themselves a self-blaming story as long as they possibly can if it helps keep cognitive dissonance at bay. And in America that is a very long time, because our hyper-individualistic culture blinds us to forces beyond the control of, well, an individual. But when enough evidence accumulates that the game is truly crony-rigged, and that merit and effort have little to do with ascent, that justice is not blind but instead winks at the powerful, there comes a forceful snap-back to reality. Literally, a dis-illusionment.

The pain of such awakenings can be converted to action and reform—as during the American Revolution or the civil rights movement—or it can lead to an utterly paralyzing cynicism. We are in a world of such pain today. The key variable now is whether citizens will remember how to claim power. That's not as easy as it sounds. It begins with remembering that claiming is *possible*. Hence our third law of power.

LAW 3: POWER IS INFINITE

In politics, power is usually seen as a zero-sum game—your gain has to be my loss, because there's a fixed amount of power in the system. But that is a law of thermodynamics, not civics. Citizens in fact *can* create power out of thin air—without taking it from anyone else—and often do. There is no limit on the amount of power in a polity. Power is positive-sum, not zero-sum.

That is because power emerges from the imagined as much as from the material. In fact, it emerges first from the imagined. The material sources of power—whether violence or bureaucratic pressure or financial incentive—are only the manifestation of what is imagined. And in situations that seem like a win-lose conflict, it is often possible to create win-win outcomes—if the parties are willing to imagine them.

I know the idea that power is infinite and positive-sum sounds like a Pollyanna, New Age promise that's of little use to a young black man in a traffic stop or to a fast-food server with a sick child and a late shift or to a laid-off textile worker whose job went to Vietnam twenty years ago. And there are some situations—such as a presidential election—where the choices are mutually exclusive and the game is truly zero-sum. But the claim that power is infinite is in fact pure realism. Every activist who has ever had to engage forces of superior power knows it—indeed, relies on it, in order to alter the terms of the engagement.

What does it mean for power to be infinite? There is a metaphysical answer to the question, which I'll return to. But let's start with a very practical and very local answer.

In the prosperous Chicago suburb of Glenview, retiree Nancy Mullarkey read in the paper one morning that the town Board of Trustees had passed an ordinance allowing landlords to refuse to rent to low-income people who were using housing vouchers. An active member of a church whose slogan was "A house for all God's people," Mullarkey decided she had to act. She organized her church's Faith in Action group, which linked up with a fair-housing nonprofit and the League of Women Voters. Together they launched a repeal campaign, writing letters to local newspapers and board members.

The fight was controversial: landlords complained about interference, neighbors warned of crime. After a year of pressure, the ordinance came up for a repeal vote in early 2015. Fifteen members of Mullarkey's church showed up to speak at the meeting. The trustees voted to repeal, five to one. Two more meetings were needed to ratify the repeal, and more advocates came to those until the repeal was finalized. "If you don't act on what you believe in," Mullarkey said later, "you're not going to live in the society you want to live in. And you can be effective. You can make change."

When Mullarkey first read that newspaper article, there was a particular array of power in Glenview, dominated by landlords, affluent neighbors, and the trustees. When she organized members of her church, she changed that array by creating additional power.

Here are another couple of examples. In February 2006, months after Hurricane Katrina, Mayor Ray Nagin of New Orleans signed an executive order creating a new landfill—named Chef Menteur—to hold post-storm debris. It was to be located just two miles from the neighborhood of Versailles, home to over 6,000 Vietnamese Americans. This was ominous for Versailles, where elderly residents had spent years gardening in nearby wetlands, growing sugar cane, bitter melon, and other vegetables. The state environmental agency ruled that safeguards to prevent seepage of toxic contaminants were unnecessary, and that the Katrina emergency necessitated a new landfill. Chef Menteur officially opened in April.

Over the next few months, however, young and elderly Vietnamese American residents staged protests at City Hall and the landfill site itself. They were joined by African American community leaders from the Ninth Ward. Environmental activists pushed for testing of the landfill soil and moved a bill through the state legislature to redirect debris to an already existing landfill. By August, the city government, outflanked by citizens at every turn, chose not to renew the landfill's permit. Chef Menteur was stopped, and Versailles saved.

When Robyn Twemlow of Christchurch, New Zealand, learned in 2013 that her nine-year-old daughter, Analise, had Tourette syndrome, she felt utterly alone. She searched for a support group and found nothing. So she took to social media and found a friend of a friend whose child also had Tourette's. Then Robyn, a former journalist, was emboldened to reach out to the local paper in search of other families in the same situation. The response was overwhelming. From around the country and across demographics came stories of exhausted families, all thinking they were alone.

Robyn decided to act. She formed the Tourette's Association of New Zealand to provide support, education, and advice—and perhaps more fundamentally, to make a community out of people who were experiencing identical struggles in isolation. The association launched "Camp Twitch," a joyful face-to-face convening for children, parents, and adults ("tic loud, tic proud, and give a tic").

Now Robyn has become an organizer of families living with Tourette's. She pushes elected officials for policy changes and funding to address the physical and mental aspects of the disorder. She works the media to increase public understanding and to reduce bullying. In her case, as in the others, organizing other people is the key variable.

So when I say power is infinite, I mean it can be conjured up almost magically by organizing. *Organizing is magic.* It is magic in that it creates something from seemingly nothing, without subtracting from what existed previously. When you teach me to give a speech in public, you add to the amount of activated power in the world. You do not subtract power from people who already knew how to do public speaking.

But there are two words I just used that I want to call your attention to: *seemingly* and *activated.* It only *seems* like power is being created out of nothing when organizing is under way, but what truly is happening is that previously dormant power is being awakened and *activated.* In other words, the dormant power was there all the time.

This brings us to the more metaphysical sense in which power is infinite. Power is what we allow it to be. If we don't allow ourselves to be intimidated or frozen by another party's wealth or muscle or morality, if we remember the unlimited reserves of power within each of us—and within us collectively—then we change the math of power. Smalls can become equal to, or greater than, the large.

This becomes clear in cases of nonviolent disobedience, when underdogs challenge the power structure by ostentatiously *removing* a form of their power from the equation. When you passively resist arrest at a protest, you are denying yourself the opportunity to use the form of power called violent force, even as an agent of the state's monopoly on force is arresting you. In that moment you gain power—more power than you would have had if you had physically resisted.

The same is true when a group of people boycott. Denying a business or a class of businesses the benefit of your money is an exercise of your power. You don't have to be wealthy to have an impact. You just have to have a lot of other non-wealthy people similarly willing to stop giving their power away to the business.

By deliberately withholding power, you generate more. By choosing to redirect it, you remember that the choice is yours. Such acts remind us how much dormant civic power we actually have—and how infrequently we ever activate that potential in full.

Many millions of people today feel stuck in a state of inequality and insignificance. But feeling stuck isn't the same as being stuck. Even in the most static situations we can find reminders of our own agency—and responsibility.

As a clever billboard I once saw on a congested highway put it: "You aren't stuck in traffic. You *are* traffic."

Let that sink in. We aren't stuck in broken politics, rigged economics, and a coarsening culture. We *are* these things. We have authored them, over generations, by our actions and omissions. And we can now reimagine and rewrite them, dramatically.

This means we are all complicit in every inequity we experience. We are co-creators of our own prisons, mental and physical.

SHEE
CHR
xxxxxxxx5857
11/19/2020

Item: 0010090587121 ((book)

To put it in the affirmative: we are co-authors of our own liberation. And that liberation is a non-zero, positive-sum experience.

Susan B. Anthony and the suffragette movement proved this. Granting the franchise to women did not nullify the votes of men or weaken the male sex generally. True, it did curtail the ability of men to legislate for women as if they were helpless children incapable of self-government. And that may have *felt* to some men like a diminution of relative power. But in absolute terms and actual fact, it was a boost of power for *everyone*. By making the entire polity and society more representative and inclusive, women's suffrage ensured that every American had become a more powerful member of a more powerful nation, one more adaptive and resilient in the face of all challenges.

HOW THESE LAWS PLAY OUT

So let's recap the three laws of civic power that I've described. Power concentrates. Power justifies itself. Power is infinite.

The cycle of monopoly and monopoly busting that emerges from these three laws is on vivid display in our politics today, both in the United States and around the world. When the cycle stalls after Law 2—after concentrated power has justified and entrenched itself—we get the all-too-familiar ills of our society: structural racism and sexism, race-to-the-bottom economics, mass incarceration of brown and black men, crony capitalism, bureaucratic bloat, unaccountable representatives. Worse, we get a mass epidemic of learned helplessness among the people.

But when events and catalytic leaders remind us of the truth of Law 3—that those getting a raw deal can create a new deal by looking beyond the confines of their helpless situation and *making more power*—then we get the ferment of these times.

What looks like anger and disillusionment today among so many bottom-up movements—from the Tea Party to striking fast-food workers, from young Sanders fans to angry white Trump supporters, from Black Lives Matter to Moms Demand Action for Gun Sense in America, from campus social justice activists to campus free-speech champions—is in fact a deeply optimistic surge. True alienation is deadly silent and sullen. The upheaval and ruckus of our times are hopeful at heart. People still believe change is possible.

Consider the politics of criminal justice.

For over a generation, there was a consensus across party lines that policy makers needed to be "tough on crime." The only question was how tough was tough enough. So "three strikes you're out" laws were enacted. Stop-and-frisk policies were put into place. Penalties for drug use and commerce were stiffened. Mass incarceration was the predictable result. And from there, the emergence of a prison-industrial complex in which private prison operators and unions representing prison workers became major political donors and players. Public budgets flowed increasingly to corrections. Police tactics became increasingly militarized. And the impacts fell overwhelmingly on communities of color, especially African Americans.

This was a case study of the concentration and compounding of power. What started as a race-colored reaction to rising crime became a self-justifying and self-perpetuating institutional latticework. A code of solidarity within law enforcement, a policing culture that valued aggression over compassion, electoral incentives that made politicians and prosecutors ignore the grievances of minority communities, a narrative that police brutality and mass incarceration were the price to pay for low crime, and financial rewards for criminalizing everyday behavior and expanding the reach of prisons—all added up to a conspiracy of silence about the injustices of the criminal-justice system.

Although the "tough on crime" consensus seemed fixed, there was from the start a contest over its effectiveness and legitimacy. The challenges played out in opinion journals and think tanks, on street corners and in city halls. The forces of critique and dissent were initially isolated and marginal, but they understood that it is possible and necessary to unfreeze a policy consensus both by attacking it and by proposing alternatives. Works like Michelle Alexander's *The New Jim Crow* were devastatingly effective at awakening citizens and helping them imagine a different state of affairs.

And even though it appeared nobody was in charge of unwinding the prison-industrial complex, an ecosystem of activists was in fact emerging, from uncoordinated points across the country, and mobilizing. All of them recognized that even in the face of such a seemingly immovable power structure, they could generate new power of their own.

They were aided by a combination of circumstances. On the right, fiscal conservatives began to chafe at the huge budget outlays for policing and prisons in local budgets. Libertarians resented the rise of a police state that used predatory fines and civil asset forfeiture to fund its operations on the backs of the poor. On the left, social-justice activists awakened the public to the "school-to-prison pipeline" that sucked brown and black youth into systems of discipline that led ultimately to incarceration. Activists on all sides were motivated by their own ideological reasons to act.

Then in August 2014, the killing of Michael Brown by a police officer in Ferguson, Missouri, sparked protests around the country. Thus began a new era of heightened scrutiny and moral outrage not only about police misconduct but also the way the justice system generally is skewed to make black lives and black dignity matter less.

Now a diverse coalition for change has coalesced. Progressives turned the hashtag #BlackLivesMatter into a rallying cry and the basis for a reform agenda that is broader than police practice and focuses on the carceral state generally. Conservatives and libertarians in Texas and other red states launched a movement to be "right on crime" rather than just tough on crime. Protesting and lobbying, activists have thrust these issues onto the national consciousness, forcing presidents, pastors, police chiefs, and everyday people to face them more squarely—and to make changes in law and custom.

That said, the outcome of this loose reform coalition remains uncertain. Though there are unprecedented levels of bipartisan cooperation today on criminal-justice reform, the fact is that most people aren't clued in to this issue, most aren't willing to fight for change, and plenty of interests, from individual politicians to corrections unions or prison contractors, will opportunistically organize for counterreformation. Meanwhile, the debate over policing has become more sharply polarized by continued police killings—and by the murder of police officers in Dallas, Baton Rouge, and elsewhere.

If reform activists are to succeed, they will have to demonstrate both in their storylines and in their policy proposals that power is positive-sum—that changing criminal penalties and policing procedures does not mean, in a zero-sum way, that bad guys will now get to run rampant or that the lives of policemen don't matter; but rather, that when a system of justice treats all citizens with fairness and respect and not like an occupied population, the entire society grows stronger. The once-occupied become true citizens. The onetime occupiers do, too. Everyone is humanized.

It's not an easy sell. But protesters don't have to get a majority of the public to win. During the civil rights movement, large majorities of the public thought that Freedom Rides and lunch-counter sit-ins and marches across militarized bridges were counterproductive, and that reform was moving too quickly and disruptively. Today, all those tactics have been sanctified in national memory. All that has to happen for the criminal-justice reform movement to succeed today is this: a catalytic minority must cohere—and be willing and able to shape the frame of the politically possible.

Remember where we began in this discussion: power is a gift.

At every turn of the cycle here—the consolidation of power in the prison-industrial complex; the justification of that power in ideologies about crime, punishment, race, and morality; and the upending or bypassing of that structure by reform activists—power is being given. That is true of those whose inaction or inattention passively legitimizes a "tough on crime" status quo. But it is also true of those who actively support such a regime—as well as those who actively seek an alternative.

We are all giving power to others by our actions and omissions. When we surrender it unmindfully or heedlessly, our power

tends to gravitate toward reinforcing the status quo. When we circulate it intentionally, we can direct it as we choose, whether for
change or against it. Then we become engaged in a contest over
legitimacy.

What is legitimacy? What ultimately makes the exercise of
power legitimate? That's the topic of the next chapter.

LEGITIMACY AND THE POWER STRUCTURE

INCLUSION AND LEGITIMACY

In 1969, twelve American women, ranging from twenty-three to thirty-nine years old, met for a workshop about taking control of their own health care. Out of their frank and cathartic conversations about how male physicians treated them, they formed what became the Boston Women's Health Book Collective.

The collective exchanged ideas and soon compiled a 193-page stapled pamphlet on "Women and Their Bodies," which explored subjects such as sexuality and abortion that weren't generally part of public discourse. The buzz about the pamphlet was intense, and soon the group had retitled it and published it as a book: *Our Bodies, Ourselves*. The rest is herstory. The book became a catalytic part of a movement to liberate women with knowledge and community; millions of copies later, it changed the world.

In the medical profession, power from the beginning was concentrated in the hands of men. The monopoly was justified by a variety of forces: social norms of deference to white men in white coats; interlocking directorates of medical schools and associations dominated by men; intellectual paradigms establishing the male body as the default for the practice of medicine. Against that array, the members of the Boston Women's Health Book Collective appeared to have little countervailing power. But they generated it by organizing. By organizing people, ideas, money, and information, they shifted the very basis of *legitimacy* in health care.

Legitimacy is the widespread belief that institutions of power are just, both in their origins and operations, and should thus be respected. Slow to accumulate, legitimacy can be very quick to evaporate. What makes revolutionary times revolutionary—whether in the 1770s or 1960s or today—is that long before people make decisions to put their bodies and voices in the path of the powers that be, they've made a judgment that the system is no longer legitimate.

In American politics, power is presumptively *illegitimate*. It's important to remember this. Our founding is premised on the notion that power is inherently hostile to freedom. The pamphlets of the Revolution are heavy with warnings that citizens must "jealously" guard their liberties against tyrannies of the state. The Constitution, even as it created a stronger national government, hobbled that government with checks and balances, separations of power, local prerogatives, and deliberate ambiguities meant to be resolved in favor of the people.

So if power has always been suspect here, on what basis does it truly earn legitimacy in America? On this basis only: *inclusion*. From hatred of "taxation without representation" to passion for "equal protection of the law," we Americans have believed in and preached inclusion. Even when we have failed to practice it.

Maybe that's because we've had a strong gut sense of how to survive. The evolutionary logic of social and institutional inclusion is pretty simple. Diverse groups that figure out how to cooperate outperform and outlast groups that don't. There is a mountain of social science behind that statement. Cooperation, in turn, is the product of inclusion. Social virtues such as trust and generosity and compassion may seem like they're for suckers, but in fact they're for winners. They help groups cohere in ways that enable all members to survive and thrive, and the group to endure.

The United States at its best—in the first decade after the Civil War, or in the generation after World War II—has been this kind of society. During these times in particular, the nation put muscle behind its stated creed of equality and liberty. It made citizens of people who had been enslaved or alien. It gave these former outsiders a piece of the action—not just materially but also politically. And it was this sharing of power that enabled the society to adapt, evolve, and thrive—compared to the status quo ante, certainly, and also compared to contemporary rivals. Inclusion made our society's power structure more legitimate, which made our society stronger.

But if that is so, why do so many communities and organizations today ignore the logic of inclusion? Why do we forget the story? Because humans are by nature shortsighted, and because it is hard to sustain multigenerational checks against our own nature.

The generation that rebuilt the world after 1945 knew how important it was for America at that pivotal moment not to hoard its unprecedented power but to recirculate it, through the Marshall Plan for a starving and shattered Europe, through the reconstruction of Japan, through the creation of the International Monetary Fund and the World Bank and other development institutions that *by their design* would eventually end American postwar monopoly and create more economic competitors—and partners—for the United States. That set of rules worked.

But memory is short. Now the generations with no experience of the circumstances that necessitated the rules see only their downsides. They feel taken advantage of. They want to repeal the postwar world. Hence the Brexit. Hence the unwinding of the EU. Hence Trump's disavowal of America's NATO commitments.

At home, the same postwar period for the same reasons saw the creation of rules to empower workers and to curb corporate greed and self-dealing. That set of rules worked, too: the 1950s and 1960s saw the emergence of a mass middle class and prosperity for the many. By the late 1970s, though, a new generation emerged, forgetting the mutuality of the past and seeing only that short-term profits weren't being maximized. This cohort repealed the rules, with bipartisan gusto. They undermined unions, deregulated corporations, and unleashed finance with the economic collapse of 2008, with today's political upheaval the eventual outcome.

Such is the cycle of human shortsightedness. So it falls to each generation to state anew the case for rules that will prevent winner-take-all hoards and monopolies from knocking the whole system over. We also have to update those rules, so that what was designed for the greater good doesn't harden into special benefits for a few. We have to *choose* to circulate power collectively if we want to fulfill our potential individually.

This usually involves a fight.

In a previous book, *The Gardens of Democracy*, I articulated with my co-author, Nick Hanauer, a contrast between the "trickle-down" theory of economics and what we called a "middle-out" theory. Trickle-down economics says the rich are "job creators" who must be coddled in the tax code and economic policy so that their wealth can make its way down to the rest of us. Middle-out economics says that the working and middle classes are the real job creators. It's *their* demand that powers a great economy and it's from *their* paychecks that the system generates lasting prosperity. To put it simply: When workers have more money, businesses have more customers. A virtuous cycle begins.

You can read *Gardens* for the full exposition of middle-out economics. Suffice it to say that there is also such a thing as middle-out citizenship. What is true of economic prosperity is true also of civic flourishing. We are flourishing civically when every *potential* participant actually does participate to his or her fullest and thrives. When citizens have more power, institutions have more participants. A virtuous cycle begins.

In civically flourishing societies, the people remember that the system is healthiest and most robust when power emerges from the bottom up and the middle out, not the top down. In such societies, the people recognize that it is not only *fair* that power be circulated widely; it is also *wise*. Wise, in the sense that an ounce of prevention is worth a pound of cure. Wise, in the sense that when more people are more invested in the health of the society for more of their lives, we set in motion a positive feedback loop of liberty and responsibility and creativity.

That's not how it looks to incumbents and monopolists. They think their self-interest lies in hoarding and sustaining the compounding benefits of Laws 1 and 2. Fortunately, though, this is a moment in America and around the planet when great numbers of people are ready to remake the power structure.

YOU AND THE POWER STRUCTURE

Just what is a power structure? In his classic 1956 book *The Power Elite*, the sociologist C. Wright Mills imagined the power structure as an overlapping set of military, corporate, and political leaders who were able to rule over an industrialized mass citizenry. Similarly, the political scientist G. William Domhoff answered the title of his book *Who Rules America?* by identifying both a general ruling class of corporate wealth and specific individuals who run companies and universities and exclusive associations.

But there's another way of thinking about power structures that is focused less on rulers and more on systems. Not because rulers—the elite—don't deserve our suspicious attention. They do.

But because when we talk about a "power structure" it can help to imagine an actual structure: a 3D map of conduits that channel the flow of power in various directions from various sources.

Here are some of the main sources of power:

- *Violence* and physical force. Control of the means of force—whether in the police, a militia, or a gang—is power at its most primal.
- *Wealth*, which creates the ability to buy results—and to buy almost any other kind of power. Wealth is power at its most convertible.
- *State action.* This is the use of bureaucracy to compel people to do or not do certain things. It's backed by force, if needed, but depends more on legitimacy.
- *Ideas*—individual liberty, say, or racial equality—can move legislators, armies, and dollars.
- *Social norms*, or what other people think is OK. Norms don't have the centralized machinery of government, but they can certainly make people change behavior— and even change laws.
- *Numbers.* Lots of humans. A vocal mass of people creates power by expressing collective intensity of interest. Numbers express legitimacy—and can thus challenge incumbent ideas of legitimacy.

And here are some examples of conduits of power:

- *Institutions.* An institution is a persisting pattern of complex, collective behavior. The institution of marriage is one example; the institution of segregation another. Constitutional monarchy. The scientific method. Baseball. All have rules, rituals, and arenas that participants implicitly agree upon and sustain.

- *Organizations* are the operating units of institutional action. They can have official trappings of state recognition, like corporations. Or be utterly unofficial like social movements or insurrections.
- *Networks* are platforms for organizing, communicating, and building power. Technology, like social media today or printed pamphlets 240 years ago, creates one kind of network. Shared identity—from gender to class to race to alumni status—yields another. Affinity can direct the flow of power as powerfully as technology.
- *Law* is the set of incentives and disincentives, rewards and punishments, that shape our public actions. It can take the form of written or unwritten codes.
- *Narrative* includes ideology, propaganda, and political or cultural values. Patriotism is a classic form of narrative that can direct citizen power.

As I said earlier about the three laws of power, I make no pretense that these lists are exhaustive, or that the line between sources and conduits is bright and fixed. You can add to the lists or scramble them. But when you overlay the sources of power and the conduits as I've described them, and you apply the resulting framework to a particular environment, the architecture of power there becomes clearer.

SEEING IN SYSTEMS

To look for these sources and conduits of power clearly is to begin to see in systems. Revolutionaries see in systems. The founding generation of leaders did. So did the leading members of the civil rights generation. So did the most effective abolitionists and pro-hibitionists and suffragettes. So have the architects of the conservative movement since the mid-twentieth century. As well as the pioneers of LGBTQ liberation movements around the world. And so did Lech Walesa and Solidarity in Poland, Mahatma Gandhi in India, Václav Havel in what became the Czech Republic.

Seeing in systems means focusing not on isolated aspects of events or environments but on how things connect. Systems thinking reflects the complex, dynamic interdependence of life. It is a rejection of what Francis Fukuyama has called "the Hobbesian fallacy" of pure autonomy and self-reliance. It is a realization that to exercise power is not only or always to control or to direct; it is also and as often to yield, to ride a wave, to anticipate a convergence. It is to understand networks.

Many of us already do systems thinking on an intuitive level. When I asked a group of fifth graders once for examples of systems in their lives, they intuitively grasped the idea immediately. One said: the way water gets to our water fountains in school. Another chimed in: the way our favorite cereal gets to the Safeway. A third, cutting closer to the core: why my bus service got cut but my friend's didn't. I was surprised at their sophistication, but perhaps I shouldn't have been. Humans evolved to see in systems. And as I've posed these questions to adults, whether veterans or immigrants or teachers or neighborhood activists, they all get it as well.

But increasingly, what they also get is that the systems we have today—for allocating resources, for cultivating talent, for generating prosperity, and for governing ourselves—are in decay. We need new systems that provide more of us with more dignity and more control over our own lives. Getting these new systems will take a conceptual revolution no less significant than the ones that attended the birth of this nation.

There is no such thing as a neutral human system. There is no such thing as an apolitical process. Every human system is evidence of human preference or bias. Every human system is evidence of choices made—and forfeited—about how to allocate and distribute power. Facebook's system for deciding what stories are deemed "trending" in its News Feed is run partly by algorithms but also by human editors and curators. Conservatives complain those editors have a left-wing bias—and even the supposedly neutral algorithms are of course made by humans with bias, conscious or not.

The body of judge-made law that gives our Constitution life is partly the product of highly technical tests and universal axioms applied to particular circumstances. But all those jargon-filled tests and axioms were fashioned by humans with bias. Constitutional law is not primarily an expression of justice; it is primarily an expression of power: who has the power to define "liberty" or "equal protection" or "speech" one way rather than another and to make that definition synonymous with "justice."

The Federal Reserve, which manages the money supply of the country and thus a great portion of the global economy, is similarly driven by highly arcane and technical formulas that have the whiff of science and that appear, like mathematics, to rise above grubby human preferences or biases. Don't kid yourself. The Fed's decision-making—about whether to focus on fighting inflation and asset bubbles or on boosting employment and wages— is the product of contests over power, between Wall Street and workers' advocates, between neoclassical economists and Keynesians. That's why savvy activists today are trying to break open the closed meetings of the Fed and make it more susceptible to citizen pressure. Some want to "End the Fed" altogether.

When we remember that no system is God-given, we remember that every system is changeable. Which means every system has already been changed, more than once.

Consider the case of humble hair braiders. All across the United States, stylists in modest storefront salons offer the service of African-style hair braiding. Often they are immigrants or people of color, as are their clients. But in many states, occupational regulations make it illegal for hair braiders to make money practicing this trade unless they first enroll in and pay for hundreds of hours of mandatory cosmetology courses. In 2014, the Institute for Justice, a libertarian public-interest law firm, launched a national Braiding Initiative to challenge these rules as unduly burdensome and anti-competitive.

A movement has arisen beyond braiding, and beyond just right-of-center activists, to challenge licensure requirements more widely in jobs ranging from dog trainers to casket sellers. Because these regulations often govern low-skilled, low-income occupations, many of the practitioners pushing for change have long operated in isolation and civic poverty. Now they are getting activated and organized. Some progressives, concerned that licensure rules can depress wages and raise prices, are joining the push for reform or repeal. In 2015, the Obama administration proposed funding an effort to streamline such rules. From Minnesota to Texas, North Carolina to Washington, hair braiders are gaining advocates and clout.

To be sure, state regulators, professional trade associations, and public health advocates have defended the licensure requirements and lobbied against proposed changes. But a broad alliance has emerged on behalf of everyday Americans to fight what can be framed as economic and political monopoly. Every conduit of power is in play—from narratives about unshackling job creation, to the incentive structures by which professions control entry, to organizations that can challenge the very institution of occupational regulation. And the hair braiders themselves (or the animal massagers or manicurists) are getting a real-time education in how to change a power structure.

Now think about how the same systems and structures of power play out in a particular *place*.

East Ramapo is a town in the outer suburbs of New York City with an Orthodox Jewish majority and a black and Latino minority. Orthodox leaders have taken over the local school board. They've methodically disinvested in the public schools, whose students are predominantly black and Latino, and funneled taxpayer dollars to Orthodox private schools. This has been going on for years. The state Board of Regents has called on the legislature to replace the local board. But nothing's happened. And the families of the black and Latino students have not yet mobilized effectively.

A damning report in *Bloomberg Businessweek* showed how the Atlanta Braves baseball team gets small towns in the Deep South to build them lavish minor league stadiums. The Braves organization pits town against town, extracting concessions ruthlessly, so that the "winning" town ultimately ends up footing the bill for the stadium, getting little of the promised economic benefit and falling so deeply into debt that it has to cut public services. It's a little game the Braves play. And in the towns that get the ballparks, like Pearl, Mississippi, elected officials are frustrated and browbeaten and the citizens often oblivious to the cost of the deal until municipal budgets get slashed.

In Twin Falls, Idaho, a university runs a program to resettle refugees from around the world. It's been going for decades. When refugees from the war in Syria begin to arrive in 2015, though, a group of local citizens mobilized to protest their arrival—citing the threat of ISIS and terrorists coming to the United States. They organized to qualify a ballot initiative that would ban refugee resettlement in the city. A different group of citizens then organized in response, forming a committee called the Magic Valley Refugee Advocates. They fought the ballot measure and activated other communities—from Mormon congregations to university leaders to law enforcement—to join their cause.

What's the power structure in each place? Who has to be moved or mobilized to change the situation? What systems can you influence and what systems will you have to bypass altogether?

To return to the central question of civic life and legitimacy: *Who decides?*

Whenever groups of citizens try to generate new power on their own, what they are trying to do specifically is to change, influence, or replace the conduits around them. For that, there is ultimately no substitute for practice. Which is to say, experience.

EXPERIENCE MATTERS MOST

Although I often disagree with him on policy, I have learned a lot from Matt Kibbe, the former Tea Party activist at FreedomWorks and the founder of Free the People, a new cross-partisan libertarian group targeting millennials. Matt and his compatriots have recognized from the start that they must always be taking the initiative, that when they sit back and let others define and caricature them, as happened with the presidential candidacies of both Ron and Rand Paul, their cause is weakened.

So in addition to preaching the virtues of libertarianism, these activists have been relentless about finding and forcing national policy fights. The fight might be to defund the Export-Import Bank, or to bring an end to civil asset forfeiture, or to curtail NSA surveillance, or to dismantle the Federal Reserve. Each fight, whatever the outcome, generates power because it creates a focal point for organizing. Their motive is liberty.

But of course, Kibbe and his colleagues also care deeply about the actual outcomes. Whether the Ex-Im Bank becomes a casualty of their assault on "crony capitalism" is not of academic interest: they want to win. And they want to win because they see a government—in what Madison called the "encroaching nature of power"—that is intervening ever more actively in our economic and private lives. They push back against relentless state encroachment, and they organize the young, on campuses and in hubs of innovation like Silicon Valley, speaking a language of freedom that is not moldy and boring but is open, inviting, and even exciting.

Now consider another group of activists. These are the Dreamers—young people born outside the United States, brought here illegally as children, who have decided to come out openly as undocumented and to claim their place in America. They earned their name by championing the DREAM Act, which would give people like them a pathway to citizenship if they served in the military or went to college. But they also are pushing for broader reforms to our immigration system. They've put themselves on the line, risking deportation. This is the only country most have ever known and loved.

Cristina Jimenez founded the largest advocacy group for undocumented youth, United We Dream. She and her allies have deployed every source of power I described above: crowd power (massive rallies in cities across the country), wealth power (support from venerable philanthropies), ideas power (using social media to make deeply compelling personal videos), norms power (simply by coming out of the shadows and asserting and normalizing their presence).

But at the heart of their work, Cristina and her army of Dreamers have focused on government action. When comprehensive immigration reform stalled in Congress, they pressured President Obama to issue executive orders to give people who would have qualified under the DREAM Act temporary relief from deportation. That was a win (though it was subsequently challenged in the courts). At the same time, Obama continued deporting undocumented people who didn't qualify as Dreamers—indeed, to show his "rule of law" bona fides, Obama deported more immigrants than any prior president. That was a setback for the movement.

To the Dreamers, state action is therefore not an unqualified good or evil. It works to protect them, and it works to threaten them—especially now. These advocates are motivated to win because the unity of their families and the scope of their own opportunities depend on winning. Their motive is justice.

What Matt's limited-government libertarians and Cristina's social-justice progressives share is a motivation that extends beyond the words "liberty" and "justice." They share a vision of a society where more people are able to claim and create more power—for themselves, by themselves—against the encroachments of others. And they now share an *experience* that teaches them that it is both possible and necessary to create power: to activate people who very reasonably could believe that the deck is so stacked against them that there's no point in getting involved.

The philosophical tradition of pragmatism holds that the worth of our beliefs—about power, about identity, or anything—should be measured by their actual usefulness in action. That is what the American pragmatist philosopher William James called the "cash-value" of an idea. When experience shows us that a belief in something yields positive and useful outcomes, we will hew to that belief. We will imagine it to have causal power. And by so imagining, we will—for all practical purposes—make it so.

So it's not enough to understand power. Or to have beliefs about it. We have to *experience* it, even the slightest taste.

As we've seen, it is in the nature of power structures—and of complex adaptive systems generally—for advantage and disadvantage to beget more advantage and disadvantage. What *theoretically* separates a democracy from a plutocracy or an oligarchy is that in a democracy we are supposed to have circuit breakers in place: ways to interrupt the loop of unearned compounding advantage.

People on the right and left today agree that in practice the circuit breakers are not working. We agree that our political and economic systems—the markets of ideas and of goods that are supposed to give us meaningful, empowering choices—have become corrupt at the core. Unfortunately, each ideological group has a big blind spot when it comes to detecting concentrated power. Liberals do not see government overreach; conservatives do not see corporate overreach.

What if right and left could merge their half-blind perceptions and create a more truly binocular sense of the political system? What if more people, equipped with an understanding of how all the elements of power in civic life come together, used that binocular vision to challenge monopoly and the hoarding of power in all its forms?

The framers of the Constitution—having read ancient history, contemplated moral philosophy, and *experienced* a revolution and a failed confederation—brought to the task that kind of binocular vision. *The Federalist Papers* makes for bracing reading today: Hamilton, Madison, and Jay had an exceedingly clear-eyed view of human nature. They understood that self-love and love of power are immutable human tendencies; that such tendencies mean all societies bend toward corruption and tyranny; that the purpose of government is to safeguard our liberty and yet that government itself can threaten liberty; and therefore that power must be set against power in unending contest so no single interest can ever dominate.

At the same time, they preached *responsibility*. Indeed, Madison essentially re-coined it. Until the Revolution, notes the historian Charles Kesler, that rarely used word connoted response or responsiveness. The *Federalist* authors gave "responsibility" a new meaning: authority coupled with *accountability*. But timeless as their insights were, the *Federalist* authors overestimated how much responsibility future generations would actually be willing to take. And they did not foresee how much a mass society—mass capitalism, mass government, mass elections—would make citizens believe themselves to be small and insignificant: *unworthy* of responsibility.

This is where experience matters. Experience makes us mistrustful of fads that say "power is over" or that power has been reinvented. Experience teaches us that power will flow in novel ways as society evolves and becomes more complex, but that the animating *force* of power—the human will for desired outcomes—is constant. And experience reminds us that the belief that we are unworthy of power or responsibility is one of the most rapidly self-fulfilling beliefs there is.

For several generations running, most Americans have not had an experience of making positive change in social and civic life. If we were now to pen the "New Federalist Papers," based on contemporary society and our accumulated national experience, we would be tempted to rail against the failures of democracy, capitalism, and citizenship. After all, to be ruthlessly pragmatic, those ideas aren't delivering much "cash value"—literal or figurative— to the 99 percent today.

But if we were being as candid and self-critical as the framers were, we would have to admit that we haven't really tried democracy yet. We haven't really tried capitalism yet. We haven't really tried citizenship yet. And certainly not all at once.

We haven't truly enabled all the people of this society to participate in self-government to the fullest extent of their potential. We haven't come close, not in an age when our elected officials and their staffs are overwhelmingly white, male, and affluent. Nor have we truly enabled all the people of this society to participate fully in economic life as creators and contributors. Not when 48 percent of the new jobs in the country are low-wage jobs paying less than $15 an hour, and when tens of millions rely on government payments for subsistence. And we haven't truly enabled the citizens of this country to be as powerful as possible. Not when voter turnout is rarely above 60 percent (at best) and when poor, nonwhite, or immigrant voters are still being disenfranchised.

What would it look like if we truly were trying?

The patterns of corruption and disenfranchisement in American civic and economic life today are familiar to anyone who has studied the rise and fall of nations. Yet still I am optimistic. That is because, of all nations on the planet, the United States has shown a unique—call it exceptional—capacity for regeneration and renewal. For depth of corruption—moral as well as financial—and for scope of societal disease and contradiction, the period from the abandonment of Reconstruction in 1877 through the rise of the Gilded Age into the 1920s is hard to surpass. Yet this nation, with far less talent on its shores than it has today, managed to get through that period of rot.

But if we as citizens—and again, here I mean all who are willing to contribute—want to revive the promise of this experiment, we have to get more *experience*. We have to try power. We have to practice power. We have to practice making power out of thin air.

That starts with voting. Vote not just with your feet or your dollars or your "likes." Vote with your vote. You say you want a revolution? As E. E. Schattschneider wrote in *The Semisovereign People*, "All that is necessary to produce the most painless revolution in history, the first revolution ever legalized and legitimized in advance, is to have a sufficient number of people do something not that much more difficult than to walk across the street on election day."

But voting, while a central right and a vital responsibility, is really only part of practicing power. Not even the biggest part, really. To gain experience in civic power means to treat the world around us as a text to read and as a paper upon which to write. It means taking what we've covered so far about the basic elements and laws of power and applying it to actual instances of choice, conflict, coalition, and decision.

And it means, throughout, not getting wedded to any political ideology or orthodoxy except for the idea that our job now is to challenge unearned privilege, to break apart monopolies, to deconcentrate power, to make the little citizen bigger, and to fight the feeling of helplessness that gives rise to authoritarianism.

Let's explore now just how to do this.

PART III

HOW TO PRACTICE POWER

GAME, STORY, EQUATION

Now that we've examined the *what* of civic power, it's time to explore the *how*. This part of the book describes nine strategies that you can apply in civic life at every level, from the hyperlocal to the national to the global.

The strategies we'll explore here are for challengers, change agents, and disrupters. They are for people who want to claim and redistribute power.

People like Roberto Maestas.

Roberto was one of the best civic improvisers I ever knew. Born into poverty in Depression-era New Mexico and raised by his grandparents, he ran away at fourteen and became a migrant farmworker in eastern Washington State. Eventually he hustled his way west to Seattle and got himself through high school while working industrial jobs on late shifts. He eventually earned a degree in Spanish at the University of Washington and became a teacher at Seattle's Franklin High School.

It was there, during the 1960s, that his evolution into a fire-brand revolutionary began. He became a vocal leader in the emerging Chicano movement. He joined black student activist Larry Gossett, Native American leader Bernie Whitebear, and Asian American leader Bob Santos to create multiracial coalitions for justice in education, policing, immigration, and other issues. Together they became masters of organizing and direct action. The so-called Four Amigos were bonded by personal chemistry. But they also recognized that in predominantly white Seattle, they were stronger together.

This was particularly the case for Seattle's small, dispersed Latino community. Maestas sought a way to galvanize Latinos into a visible sense of shared fate. So in October 1972, he and over seventy other activists entered and took over the abandoned Beacon Hill School, which had been shuttered because of declining enrollments. The aging building lacked heat, electricity, running water, or supplies. But it now had occupants (or at least occupiers). The activists proclaimed it "El Centro de la Raza"—which they translated, strategically, as the Center for People of *All* Races.

They secured a commitment from the school superintendent that they would not be forcibly evicted, and from there they began to negotiate. As the talks got under way, the activists organized educational and artistic projects in the building, from English lessons to mural making, to show what El Centro could be. They also organized rallies at the City Council and in the streets. Along the way, Maestas and a young fellow occupier named Estela Ortega were married, in the unheated school gymnasium. Three months later, the district agreed to lease the property to the activists for $1 a year.

From that point on, El Centro became a civic hub and a political force. Combining the spirit of the urban crusader Jane Addams and the revolutionary Cuban poet José Martí, with a dose of the Black Panther Party, El Centro created a space for low-income immigrant families that was equal parts settlement house, people's school, child-care center, free breakfast program, and activist proving ground.

Maestas led with zest and swagger. He was unafraid to confront community leaders he felt weren't moving quickly enough to include poor and brown people. He marched and protested, often with the other Four Amigos. But he mastered the inside game as well. He cultivated working relationships with business and philanthropic insiders. His office became a necessary stop for aspiring political candidates.

By the time of its thirty-fifth anniversary celebration in 2007, El Centro de la Raza was serving many thousands of people annually through over forty-five different programs. It had a strong presence as an advocate for immigrants and poor communities of color. It had become a key conduit of the local power structure. Governors, mayors, councilmembers all paid homage at the anniversary, as the restless Maestas worked the room all night.

The themes undergirding this multi-decade arc of improvisation were consistent throughout: Justice. Service. Multiethnic coalition. Feisty challenges followed by subtle negotiation. Upon these chords, Roberto Maestas had started a riff in 1972—by turns playful, subtle, irreverent, indirect, aggressive—that others joined in over the years.

Roberto died in 2010 of lung cancer. Estela Ortega, who had been running things day-to-day, took over formally as El Centro's executive director. She has become a full-fledged member of the city establishment, serving on mayoral commissions and wired into City Hall. She doesn't have to raise her voice to get things done.

Ortega decided after taking over to launch a legacy project: a festive plaza, adjacent to the old schoolhouse she and Roberto had occupied so many years earlier, with street-level retail, a community center, light rail, affordable housing for hundreds of low-income residents. The project opened in 2016. It's called Plaza Roberto Maestas.

THE THREE IMPERATIVES

The story of El Centro's creation and flourishing reminds us that civic power may not require a plan—but it does require a purpose. Improvisation, when done well, is not just "winging it." It's having a set of moves that you return to over and over, that guide you as you respond to events and the people around you.

This is as true for right-wing activists who've been innovators like Newt Gingrich as it is for self-professed left-wing radicals like Maestas and his contemporaries. Indeed, the most effective civic innovators are those who take as texts the lives and methods of people quite unlike them. Across differences of style or ideology, there are deep imperatives—strategic must-dos—that every change-maker knows.

What are those imperatives? For context, let's return to our power cycle and the three core laws of citizen power:

- Power concentrates. *It creates monopolies and winner-take-all politics.*
- Power justifies itself. *It creates an all-encompassing story of its own legitimacy.*
- Power is infinite. *Yet for the most part, people think it's finite and zero-sum.*

What we're going to see now is how each of these three laws generates—practically demands—an approach to action. In just the way that the law of gravity or of diminishing returns *compels* us to adjust our actions and expectations, so do these laws of power require us to act on the world a certain way. And each one creates an opportunity for you to demonstrate that you are more powerful than you think.

So, *because*:

- Power creates monopolies, and is winner-take-all → You must change the *game*.
- Power creates a story of why it's legitimate → You must change the *story*.
- Power is assumed to be finite and zero-sum → You must change the *equation*.

These are the three imperatives of the practice of power. You change the *game* by interrupting the cycle of self-perpetuating, compounding power. This means being able to diagnose the game as it is. It means identifying just which rules are rigged to reinforce the power of those who have power and the privilege of those who get the unearned benefit of power. And it means relentlessly swarming the status quo with moves that disrupt the strategy of the status-quo powers.

You change the *story* by rewriting the social contract of the situation. That requires more than decrying the current social contract; it requires envisioning and depicting an alternative. From there, you activate or "weaponize" your alternative story of the social contract—the new deal—by using it as the basis for all your organizing. And then you pick an emblematic battle that can be understood as a fable for your entire cause.

You change the *equation* by creating power in positive-sum ways. First, you act exponentially by setting off contagions of attitude and action. Next, you design experiences of mutual aid and reciprocity that remind people of their inherent power and alert people not to give it away heedlessly. And finally, you perform power. You act it out, then change the theater of power by deploying the power of theater.

Roberto Maestas did all these things. He entered a static situation in which a marginalized community did not have voice or presence in a growing city. He changed the game with the dramatic stroke of occupying a space that was symbolically potent—an abandoned schoolhouse—and also useful as the central plaza for a movement. He and his compatriots changed the story by sharing a vision of what El Centro could be for the community and the city, and recasting the occupation not as protest but as an act of creation, of social artistry. And they changed the equation of power by directing the energy of many atomized, isolated outsiders toward mutual aid and collective self-help.

Almost any civic catalyst who makes change happen does it by changing these three imperatives of game, story, and equation.

Consider the Declaration of Sentiments. Composed principally by Elizabeth Cady Stanton and signed by sixty-eight women and thirty-two men at the Seneca Falls Convention in 1848, the Declaration is famous as the founding text of the movement for women's suffrage and women's liberation. The convention itself was an audacious attempt to change the game—to challenge a political culture and legal regime that considered men to be the creators of public life and women to be their dependents.

The document is a stellar study of changing the story—not only by depicting an alternative America where women would be equal citizens but also by deftly positioning this radicalism as conservatism. Its form and structure are deeply conservative: it is essentially an adaptation of the Declaration of Independence. The first four paragraphs track the original almost word for word, only making a few clauses gender-inclusive ("We hold these truths to be self-evident: that all men and women are created equal").

Within that conservative format, though, the message of the Declaration of Sentiments is radical to the core. The list of "sentiments," paralleling the bill of particulars indicting King George in the original, catalogs "repeated injuries and usurpation on the part of man toward woman": denial of the franchise; monopolization of most paying employment; divorce and tax laws that enforce dependence; hoarding of religious authority; and so on. And in light of these itemized forms of disenfranchisement, the Declaration—again, in homage to its antecedent—demands "immediate admission to all the rights and privileges which belong to them as citizens of these United States."

The radical-as-conservative stance is a strategy that made sense for the Seneca Falls organizers. For one thing, it calls to mind a key tactic later taught by the twentieth-century organizer Saul Alinsky: *make the other side live up to its own book of rules*. More broadly, it calls to mind Sun Tzu's advice to attack not the enemy but the enemy's *strategy*. That is the very essence of how to change a game. In a self-consciously democratic republic run by men, the core strategy of dominance is control of the meaning of "normal" citizenship. Seneca Falls contested that strategy the way a martial artist flips her opponent: by using his own energy and force against him.

But fundamentally this stance was dictated by the sober inventory these proto-feminists had taken of their own power. They had to fight with ideas and principles as their weapons—with the country's *original* ideas and principles—because at the time they did not yet have the people, the money, the allies in government, the social norms, or other sources of power. In theory they represented "one-half the people of this country," but practically they did not. So the final lines of the Declaration promise that the Seneca Falls conventioneers would now push their cause through every conduit possible: "in the pulpit and press" and in "the State and national Legislatures."

And they did. They changed the equation of power. History tells us—though it was by no means certain at the time—that by convening these activists and creating a public document that could articulate the aspirations of a movement, Stanton and her allies generated something from seemingly nothing. They set off a contagion of belief and action that would result a few decades later in the American woman's right to vote.

Change the game, change the story, change the equation. Any of us can apply this framework to any situation in our own community or field. And each of these three imperatives can in turn be unpacked to yield three strategies.

Here's how they break down.

Change the game:

    1. Adjust the arena.

    2. Re-rig the rules.

    3. Attack the plan.

Change the story:

    1. Describe the alternative.

    2. Organize in narratives.

    3. Make your fight a fable.

Change the equation:

    1. Act exponentially.

    2. Act reciprocally.

    3. Perform your power.

Together, these nine strategies form an action plan for civic change-makers. You'll realize, as we dive into each one, that Martin Luther King Jr. and Dolores Huerta and Harvey Milk and Gloria Steinem and Ronald Reagan and Ralph Reed executed all of them. You might notice Donald Trump did, too. Power is purpose-agnostic. Which is why those who become fluent in power must not be. So in the final part of the book, we will be asking the question—to what moral ends?—that any change agent must confront.

But for now, what's important to bear in mind is that these nine strategies require no prior experience, no advanced degree, no particular connections, and no inside knowledge to execute. They simply require commitment and a capacity to organize.

As I said earlier, organizing is magic. It is the foundational skill. Knowing how to meet, connect with, and make lists of potential allies; how to create private events and public experiences that bring out more friends without awakening more foes; how to listen to strangers and connect their desires and hopes with those of a larger cause; how to give everyone a simple task in a phone bank or a fund-raiser so that they can feel part of that cause— these are things that members of every PTA, student organization, civil rights group, labor union, chamber of commerce, and professional association in the country know how to do. They aren't rocket science. But they do require practice.

In the exposition of the nine strategies of civic power, I will assume you know how to do or start doing some of these microtactics of organizing. I *won't* assume that you already know how to put these tactics into a framework of strategies for collective change-making. That's what the rest of this part of the book is for.

CHANGE THE GAME

STRATEGY 1: ADJUST THE ARENA

If power concentrates, and tends toward monopoly and winner-take-all politics, then you must change the game. Our first strategy for doing that is to adjust the arena itself so that it's optimized for your situation and your relative strengths. That means deciding whether to make the arena smaller or larger; inside or outside; deep or shallow.

SMALLER OR LARGER

All civic life begins in the imagination. Imagination plus action, minus inertia, equals the world we have today. So the effective practitioner of civic power knows how to manipulate imagination—to expand or contract, as needed, the frame of the possible and the perceived scale of the fight.

To adjust the size of the arena you first must realize that the arena is yours to size. Sometimes the situation will demand that you expand the field of conflict, so that others start seeing your fight as theirs, or at least usefully linked to theirs. Other times it demands that you contract the field, so that people who might otherwise be opposed to you don't feel a need to get involved. This changes continuously.

When the city of Austin proposed a referendum in 2016 to require Uber and Lyft drivers to undergo fingerprinting and background checks, just as taxicab drivers do, Uber and its advocates chose to expand the arena aggressively.

Instead of arguing about the specifics or efficacy of background checks, Uber and Lyft framed the issue more broadly as innovation-killing government regulation of the sharing economy. They spent millions advertising against the ballot measure. Some partisan advocates, like the anti-tax crusader Grover Norquist, claimed it was a case of union-owned Democratic politicians run amok. The companies then issued an ultimatum: if the legislation passed, they would pull out of Austin altogether, stranding riders and effectively firing drivers.

The threats backfired. Austin citizens resented the bullying and passed the referendum with 56 percent of the vote. And when Uber and Lyft made good on their threat to pull out of the city, it seemed to confirm the sense of local citizens that the companies had gotten too big for their britches. Numerous start-ups have since sprung up to take what used to be Uber's business.

Throughout the campaign, referendum backers were disciplined about keeping the focus tight: this was about safety and common-sense precautions, they said. They did not attack the ride-sharing companies for adding to traffic, even though plenty of citizens were worried about that. And they did not attack the idea of ride sharing itself, which was in many ways perfectly suited to this hip, young city. They simply stuck to a principle that if taxi drivers had to go through a background check, so should Uber drivers.

It would have been far better for the ride-sharing companies had they kept a similarly tight focus and competed on the narrower question of the referendum's shortcomings. Instead, they widened the field in a way that was perceived as petulant and arrogant. They overestimated how vital they were to the city and underestimated how much the quirky, anti-establishment culture of Austin would resist their pressure.

If civic power were simply a matter of money and clout, Uber and Lyft would have prevailed. The battle of Austin reminds us not only that people power matters but also that when money and clout misread the situation, their advantages evaporate.

Another controversy shows that sometimes it's the underdog who has to expand the arena. The right-wing forces behind the anti-trans "bathroom bills" of 2016, which required transgender citizens to use public restrooms according to their gender assigned at birth, tried initially to narrow the size of the field. In their telling, the issue was specifically the risk of predatory men entering the same bathrooms as little girls.

Transgender advocates and their allies chose immediately to widen the battle. To them, this debate was about something bigger than child safety; it was about state-sanctioned discrimination. When U.S. Attorney General Loretta Lynch sued to strike down HB2, the North Carolina law, her statement was a classic example of expanding the arena:

"This is not the first time that we have seen discriminatory responses to historic moments of progress for our nation," Lynch said. "It was not so very long ago that states, including North Carolina, had signs above restrooms, water fountains and on public accommodations keeping people out based upon a distinction without a difference. . . . What we must not do—what we must never do—is turn on our neighbors, our family members, our fellow Americans, for something they cannot control, and deny what makes them human."

The battle will now play out in the federal courts. But in the court of public opinion, the strategic question is always whether and when to expand or to contract. Now that the U.S. government has sued, the backers of HB2 and similar bills can *widen* the fight to make it about states' rights and the tyranny of liberal federal social engineers. And on the ground, LGBTQ activists can now *shrink* the field and focus on empathy-stirring stories of trans people who want to live without shame. The resizing is perpetual.

INSIDE OR OUTSIDE

The next dimension of adjusting the arena to your advantage is to decide whether to play an inside or outside game. There are two meanings to this. First, whether you want the decision-making to happen in private or in public. Second, whether to identify yourself as an insider or an outsider.

A simple example of the first meaning: For a decade I served as an appointed member of the Seattle Public Library Board of Trustees. As is the case with most contemporary governmental bodies, we operated under an open-meetings law that required that any policy decision be made in public session. We strictly followed the letter of this law. Every decision—on funding, or choosing an architect to build a branch library, or whether to filter pornography on library computers—was made in meetings that had been "public-noticed" in advance, with city television cameras present.

But here's the thing: many of these choices had already been made when we called the meeting to order. Disagreements had been aired, compromises cobbled together, concerns discussed candidly—behind closed doors. These meetings before the meeting weren't official because they never contained a quorum: no more than two of the five of us would ever participate. But they were where much work got done. The *official* meeting, which included public comment periods that a few citizens would regularly avail themselves of, was often a mere ratification of decisions already taken.

This, alas, is how most public decision-making entities operate. The Kabuki staging of many public meetings is the homage we pay to our ideals of openness and transparency. But the meeting before the meeting is the concession we make to the reality that an audience often makes posturing easier and compromise harder.

Unfortunately, this way of doing business can feed public mistrust and even conspiracy theories about "the room where it happened"—the secret place where insiders cut deals against the public interest. So sometimes it becomes necessary for citizens to force the game outside: to pull the action out of those private, closed spaces and into the open.

The outside game flips—or recaptures—the stage. It makes what happens in public the true arena, and it thus circumscribes what can actually happen behind closed doors. Protest is one vivid form of the outside game, especially when it creates a spectacle that others want to watch or join. This is why Black Lives Matter matters so much: it is exposing to public view the way that police power has been wielded against black citizens, without scrutiny and with impunity.

But so is using the media to get free attention and frame issues in ways that make insider pronouncements irrelevant, as Trump did in bypassing the GOP establishment. Or exposing insider arrangements and secret deals, the way activists who are opposed to the Trans-Pacific Partnership have circulated drafts of the trade pact to highlight its most compromising compromises and to undermine it.

By shifting the action from offstage to onstage spaces, citizens can expose that which wants to hide. But it's important to point out that there is nothing inherently more worthy about one game or the other, and there is no automatic connection between underdogs and the outside game and top dogs and the inside game.

As we'll examine in depth later, there are times when the outside game is critically important—deploying the theater of politics, the publicity and visible pressure. There are other times when the inside game is key—having the safe negotiation, the room for compromise. And there are times when one game is meant to support the other. When well-organized activists flood a city-council or school-board meeting and turn it into a platform for protest or simply for compelling testimony, they are sometimes just applying enough pressure to ensure that the inside game will play out as they would like.

From the time he was a young man, Lyndon Johnson knew how to combine the inside and outside game skillfully. When he was a student at Southwest Texas State Teachers College, he was seen as an irritating, overcompensating hick outsider and was rejected by the Black Stars, the organization of "big men on campus." Stung, he joined the White Stars, the alternative organization of Black Star rejects that had a casual, nearly ironic attitude about itself. As biographer Robert Caro recounts, Johnson soon became the head of the White Stars and turned it into a secret, ruthlessly effective machine that would come to dominate campus elections and ultimately oust the Black Stars from power in student government. He used an inside game to oust the insiders.

The example of young LBJ reminds us that there is a second important meaning to inside and outside that's not about the game. It's about the players—us—and whether and when we *identify* as insiders or outsiders.

Those for whom the system works will tend to defend it. They can be quite literally invested in it. But the meaning of "for whom the system works" is multilayered and ever-changing. Johnson all his life thought of himself as an aggrieved outsider, even as he ascended to the most powerful of inside positions. Many followers of Bernie Sanders in 2016 were white, educated, and upper-middle class. Yet they wanted revolution and identified as alienated outsiders.

Meanwhile, millions of working-class right-leaning voters, for whom the economic system has decidedly not worked, have mobilized *not* around economic justice but around identity politics—religious liberty, hostility to immigration, resistance to a diversifying culture. *This* system—the cultural system that maintains straight Christian whiteness as Americanness—still "works for them," at least for the time being.

These citizens want to compensate for the reality that they've become economic outsiders with the belief that they are still identity insiders. And though demography and culture change may not be on their side, they have learned in the near term how to exercise civic power in all its forms, through its many possible conduits.

What motivates people either to accept a power structure or to decide to challenge it? What motivates them to fixate on changing one aspect of "the system" and not another? Whether *and in what sense* they identify as outsiders or insiders. What determines this is their experience. Which is never fixed.

DEEPER OR SHALLOWER

The third and final dimension of adjusting the arena is depth: deciding whether to change the institutional parameters you've inherited—or to eradicate and replace them at the root. When you are working against an entrenched power structure or in a situation where an imbalance of power has been in place for a long time, it helps to be able to distinguish between deep power and shallow power—and it is vital to decide which one is going to be the focus of your energy.

Shallow power is trying to get police departments to do better training in communities of color. Deep power is trying to disarm, defund, and demilitarize the police.

Shallow power is fighting over whether the top rate of the federal income tax should be somewhat lower or higher. Deep power is fighting to abolish the federal income tax.

Shallow power is pushing to make it less onerous to unionize non-union workplaces. Deep power is inventing brand-new *non-union* vehicles for organizing workers.

The latter is what Carmen Rojas is doing. Rojas is the executive director of the Workers Lab, a Silicon Valley–style incubator for new ventures designed to boost worker power. The Lab (on whose board I serve) takes as its premise that the New Deal framework of certified unions and collective bargaining will not be the framework of the future for most workers. That's why the Lab is supporting tools for a workforce that is increasingly low-wage, dispersed, and tech savvy: new apps that allow workers to share reports of wage theft instantly with local regulators, tech platforms that can make benefits portable or allow workers to control their own scheduling and swap shifts, and organizations that support ethically "high-road" contractors.

But the deep-power work Carmen and the Workers Lab are doing did not arise spontaneously. The Lab itself was envisioned and incubated by David Rolf, one of the top leaders at the Service Employees International Union (SEIU), who also runs a large local union in the Northwest for home-care workers. Rolf is also highly adept at the shallow-power game of pushing legislatures for higher Medicaid reimbursements or inserting provisions into omnibus laws like the Affordable Care Act that make his union members more influential.

Shallow versus deep is, in a way, about conventional versus radical politics. Except it's not really about "versus." As with the inside and the outside game, one is not inherently more appropriate or necessary, and they aren't necessarily mutually exclusive; indeed, they can feed each other.

Barney Frank, in his decades-long congressional career, learned a lot about adjusting the arena. Frank could not easily be put in a political box. As the first openly gay member of Congress, he was a civil rights pioneer. Yet he often scorned movement activists for their righteous stances. He was a deeply progressive fighter for underdogs and outsiders. At the same time, he became one of the most traditionalist defenders of government institutions, and of the system's capacity to fix itself through elections.

One of Frank's go-to phrases as a politician (with a nod to the comedian Henny Youngman) was, "Compared to what?" Whenever asked how he felt about a legislative proposal or a perhaps unsatisfying compromise, he would reply, "Compared to what?" His snarky but serious point was that politics is a choice among actionable alternatives. And the job of the powerful citizen is to put actionable alternatives on the table.

In his memoir, *Frank*, he speaks characteristically bluntly to idealistic protesters and direct-action radicals. If you're engaged in rallies or protests with like-minded people, he writes, "[y]ou are almost certainly not doing your cause any good." He felt this way during the 1970s as he was pushing housing reform as a city-council staffer in Boston, during the 1980s and 1990s as he nudged gay rights forward through the legislative process, and more recently when he took on followers of Bernie Sanders.

To the Sanders wing, for instance, the Dodd-Frank financial reform legislation is a weak law that leaves Wall Street banks far too free to gamble recklessly and to metastasize. To Frank, the primary problem with that view was not necessarily that it was wrong but that his critics, who were never able to muster the votes for the more radical reforms they preferred, never had a viable answer to the question, "Compared to what?"

Frank's realism, though, can be both his strength and his weakness. There is a necessary dialectic between shallow change and deep change, between realism and idealism. Without idealists, realists will always define progress downward. Without realists, idealists will always become insulated from responsibility for results.

During the fight for marriage equality, some activists felt that civil unions were a demeaning half measure. Others wanted to move incrementally and accept civil unions, with faith that each increment would make the next easier to secure. The truth is that both were right and that each camp needed the other. As Frank himself puts it: "Incrementalism is not the enemy of militancy; it is often the only means of expressing it." But then something like the inverse is also true: militancy is not the enemy of gradual progress; it is often the only means of achieving it.

KNOW YOURSELF

The choice for you—the citizen who wants change—is where to begin. The size, the location, and the depth of the arena are variables that you get to decide or at least influence. Don't take as given any of the givens of your situation. Read the dimensions of the arena—then understand how to change them to your benefit.

What this requires is acute awareness of oneself and one's situation.

Of the sources of power we discussed earlier (wealth, force, state action, ideas, norms, numbers), which do you have? Which can you activate most readily? Are you kidding yourself about the actual extent of your wealth or your following? Are you sure your ideas are as sticky or viral as you imagine them to be? Might you be underestimating your ability to change social norms? Does your movement rely more on elite opinion or on everyday volunteers? Is it good to rely too much on force or state action?

Political consultants often force candidates and campaigns to do a SWOT analysis—a four-box grid depicting strengths, weaknesses, opportunities, and threats—and to do a similar analysis of their opponents. That crude grid, if filled out honestly, reveals a great deal of truth. It suggests paths forward—and paths best avoided.

Arthur Brooks, the head of the conservative American Enterprise Institute, has described another simple grid he uses to locate people. The quadrants of his grid are *left*, *right*, *culture*, and *politics*. He identifies himself as right in politics, left on culture. That's because he supports free markets and small government while loving alternative rock, the Dalai Lama, and hip eyeglasses (he was raised in Seattle). He locates Gail Collins, his fellow *New York Times* columnist, as left in politics and right on culture (she was raised in a strict Catholic family).

What makes Brooks's grid more than just a conversational curiosity is that it suggests sources of power that are (and are not) available to him as an organizer, activist, and public intellectual. This unblinking form of stylistic self-knowledge—*What quadrant are you and your people in? What moral foundations move you?*—is deeply instructive.

Beyond knowing your relative strengths and weaknesses, taking a clear-eyed inventory also means understanding the extent to which the arena you have chosen can neutralize or amplify certain strengths and weaknesses.

The peripatetic Black Lives Matter activist DeRay Mckesson has over 350,000 Twitter followers. In his trademark metallic blue vest, he has appeared on the *Late Show* to explain to Stephen Colbert and the American public the meaning of his movement. He has met with President Obama and has won awards for his activism. A former New York City schoolteacher and president of his class at Bowdoin, he has a compelling presence, a clear vision, and a wide network of allies.

All of this mattered very little when he decided in 2016 to run for mayor of Baltimore. That town's parochial, relationship-based political culture not only didn't reward celebrity power; it punished it. Although he'd grown up there, Mckesson never managed to convert the currency of his global following into local capital. He mustered less than 1 percent of the vote in the Democratic primary.

But his unique assets mattered hugely several months later when he was in Baton Rouge to protest the police killing of Alton Sterling. As he walked peacefully down the street with other protesters, documenting the march live on Periscope, he was abruptly tackled by police officers and arrested without explanation. The moment was captured on video, and in a still photo of Mckesson on his knees and handcuffed, surrounded by heavily armed cops. He looks placid and determined. He is wearing a T-shirt that says #StayWoke. Both the video and the photo went viral. Soon another hashtag, #FreeDeRay, had become such a powerful call on social media that he and dozens of other protesters were released and charges dropped—and the Baton Rouge police came under even more intense scrutiny and criticism.

The protest—the live, unpredictable event that puts a premium on clarity in a crisis—was an arena that played to Mckesson's particular power profile. At the same time, he seems to have taken a lesson from his election defeat about building credibility inside the system: he announced shortly before the Baton Rouge protests that he had taken a job running human resources for the Baltimore school district.

Always adjust—and always know where you need to expand your repertoire of games.

STRATEGY 2: RE-RIG THE RULES

If power concentrates, and tends toward monopoly and winner-take-all politics, then you must change the game. The next strategy for doing this is to identify precisely the rules that have been rigged to produce monopoly—and to re-rig them for fairness.

There are two broad categories of rules to pay attention to: agenda-setting rules, and rent-seeking rules. Agenda-setting rules are those that define what is even in play and what can be considered for action. Rent-seeking rules are those that provide certain privileged people unearned, continuous advantages and benefits just for being privileged—what economists call "rents," meaning rewards without work. The key to changing both kinds of rules is transparency—and attention. You have to be able to see them. And you have to want to see them.

DECIDING, SQUARED

Civic power, whether at the level of a community council or the United States Senate, is expressed in rules of decision: *who* has the authority to decide, *what* gets considered for decision, and *how* decisions will be reached. There are limitless permutations of these rules. They can be written or unwritten. But all of them are designed to shape the agendas of our institutions.

The presidential campaigns of 2016 revealed the importance of rules of decision in both parties. From the fight over Democratic superdelegates to the too-late-in-the-day efforts of some Republicans to oust their own nominee, rule books were often front and center. But in everyday civic life in our communities or campuses, the rules are often overlooked or simply considered fixed. They are not fixed. They can be remade. First we have to see them clearly.

WHO IS AUTHORIZED TO DECIDE

Are you an elected member of a legislature, a school board, or another representative body? Are you an appointee to a commission or a regulatory council? If so, you have been formally empowered by others to decide on behalf of all.

In other cases, though, the authority is not granted formally or even lawfully; it is seized or delivered by circumstance. Have you ascended to power via coup? Are you the "power behind the throne," the aide or friend or relative of the formal decision-maker who, with that person's implied or express assent, really calls the shots? Are you perhaps the de facto leader in a group where titular power rests elsewhere?

The "who decides" question is complicated and isn't always answered by consulting the org chart. But if you are a citizen activist trying to change the rules of the system, it's important to be able to map both the formal and informal answers to the question. And then to change the map—by inserting yourself or your allies into it.

WHAT GETS DECIDED

This is a matter of what gets onto the agenda—and what doesn't. Social scientist Steven Lukes describes this as "the three faces of power." The first is the formal agenda for action, say, at a city-council meeting. *This is the docket.* The second face is what council members do *not* include on the agenda because some interest groups or powerful individuals worked hard to block or to preempt them. *This is what's between the lines of the docket.* The third face is the prevailing ideology. In a society that believes in market capitalism or white supremacy, ideology has the power to keep some things—such as "state ownership of the means of production" or "African American suffrage"—completely off the table. *This is the vocabulary of the docket.*

Being able to truly read an agenda means being able to read all three faces of rule-making power: the docket as printed; what's missing or between the lines of the docket; and the very language of the docket, which "rules in" or "rules out" certain approaches as a matter of conventional belief.

All three create opportunities for challenge. To challenge a "rigged game" at this level means to ensure that what's already on the docket goes your way and that what's not on the docket (but should be) gets placed there.

HOW DECISIONS GET EXECUTED

In much of American political life, majority rule is the default for policy making. Fifty percent plus one vote. But some decisions require a supermajority. In many states, two-thirds of the legislature or of the people themselves is required to enact a tax increase. In some, there is a 60 percent threshold for school levies.

The same variation exists for how votes are weighted. In most cases in the United States, the rule of voting is "winner-take-all." But a growing number of polities are using proportional representation or cumulative voting or ranked-choice voting to seat officeholders—all methods that allow for more than just one winner and that divide up the spoils differently.

Does all this bore you? Insiders are counting on it. This is why in almost every formal body of civic power, from a town council to a national party committee, the subgroup that is called the "rules committee" holds tremendous power—often even more than the one that appropriates money. It gets to decide how things get decided. That ability to decide on the path to decision is power, squared.

The Tea Party in 2010 was exceedingly effective at taking control of all three of these rules of decision in Congress. The movement got many long-shot outsiders elected to the House of Representatives and the Senate that November, thus dramatically changing the balance and composition of "who decides" in the federal government. Those new members then were intentional about wresting the agenda away from moderates and institution-alists who might have worked in bipartisan ways, and they put sharply ideological items like full repeal of Obamacare and the de-funding of Planned Parenthood onto the agenda. Moreover, they took radical new actions that defied the prior way of doing business in Washington, most notably refusing to raise the debt ceiling and bringing the United States to the brink of default.

Say what you will about the substance of their agenda and their ability to govern (they were generally better at obstructing and disrupting than at constructing or managing). The Tea Party adherents did appreciate the power of process. They believed that Congress had become rigged by big-government, bailout-loving, socialism-promoting Democrats and their cronies, "Republicans in name only." And they were not satisfied only to make speeches about it. They made new rules and they exploded old conventions.

Underdogs and activists of all stripes can learn something from them: namely, how to rewrite the rules you complain about.

STOP PAYING RENT

That brings us to the second set of rules, those that benefit what economists call "rent-seekers." Rent-seekers are people and institutions that leverage their power to collect wealth and advantage without any effort or social benefit.

Here's a summary of what to do about the problem: *Stop paying the rent!* But of course, it's a bit more complicated than that.

Take, for instance, the issue of arbitration. In recent years, corporations have figured out that one way to keep aggrieved customers or employees from suing them is to force those customers or employees into arbitration. Arbitration, unlike a trial, happens in private. It is decided by a single arbitrator rather than a jury of one's peers. And arbitrators, unlike judges, often derive their salary from corporations or at least from the repeat business that corporations send their way.

Sound like a rigged game? Well, wait—there's more. Given that most people would prefer an open and neutral process for resolving disputes, how do corporations manage to force so many into closed-door arbitration? Through the oldest trick in the book: fine print. In today's form of mass capitalism, we often unknowingly "assent" to all kinds of fine print when we sign up for credit cards or phone service or accept a job offer. Often that fine print says that any disputes with the seller or employer will be resolved by arbitration, by an arbitrator of the corporation's choice. Customers have no advocates up front. Workers used to, in the form of unions and collective bargaining agreements, but only a tiny fraction of the private sector is unionized now.

So most people don't realize they've been barred from using the courts—until they have cause to try. At that point, the corporations bet that disaggregated individuals won't fight this stacked system on their own, or know how to fight it collectively if class action suits are no longer an option. Corporations bet on citizen ignorance and apathy—or on worker disempowerment.

Banks and their lobbyists have quietly killed bills in California to curtail use of arbitration clauses. A bill in Congress to protect veterans from abuses of arbitration was also quashed. But labor activists, plaintiffs' lawyers, and consumer advocates have continued to organize and to challenge the rules. So when *The New York Times* began to dive deeply into this issue in recent years, making it frequent front-page news, the game began to change.

And when the federal Consumer Financial Protection Bureau began to look into the abuse of arbitration clauses, the equation shifted further. Now the CFPB, a federal agency created after the financial crisis, is developing new rules to keep consumers and workers from getting preemptively silenced. This is a great example of an attempt to re-rig the game, paying careful attention to a very specific set of practices that affect real people. But ultimately, the success or failure of this effort to will depend in good measure on how many people pay attention.

The same holds true across many sectors. Take, for example, the payday loan industry, an especially egregious case of exploitative rent-seeking. It extracts wealth from poor people, by lending money at usurious rates and entrapping borrowers in endless cycles of indebtedness. The idea, propagated by many in the industry, that they are providing credit to poor people who would not otherwise have any credit, is a form of power justifying itself. But it evades the question of why their interest rates are so high.

That's why, working in Kansas City and across the heartland, activist Eva Creydt Schulte has launched a faith-based campaign for a "moral economy." Schulte leads an interfaith coalition called Communities Creating Opportunity. A big part of CCO's work is bringing to light the religious and practical imperative of access to fair credit (among other issues of economic inclusion such as paid leave and sick leave).

Schulte elevates people like Elliott Clark, a Vietnam veteran who had to take out $2,500 in payday loans when his wife had medical expenses and ended up paying $50,000 in interest. Clark's case personifies the issue and generates media coverage. Schulte also activates a multiracial web of neighborhood and congregational groups, everyday citizens from across the region and the political spectrum. Together they have pressured state lawmakers in Missouri and Kansas to change the law (in Missouri, the maximum allowable interest rate on a payday loan is 1,950 percent, which raises the question why have limits at all). The legislatures have been unresponsive. But federal regulators have taken note, and they have come to Kansas City to hold hearings on how to rein in predatory lenders.

Game-riggers rely on the inside knowledge of experts. But sometimes, savvy citizens can use inside knowledge *against* the insiders. The carried-interest deduction in the federal tax code is a good example. This is a rule that allows hedge-fund and private-equity managers to have their income taxed not as wages but as a form of capital gains called "carried interest," which greatly lowers their tax bills. This provision is tailored to the top one-tenth of the top 1 percent. It is the very definition of rent-seeking.

In recent years, leaders ranging from Hillary Clinton to Warren Buffett to Donald Trump have called for the closing of this loophole both on principle and to recapture tens of billions of dollars of lost revenue annually. The legislation has always died in a Congress hostile to taxes and solicitous of the super-rich.

But Alan Wilensky, a former Treasury Department tax official—the kind of person who typically exits government to work for the financial industry—has suggested a way to change the rule. Go around Congress, he says. An often overlooked provision of the statute that created this form of preferential treatment allows the president simply to issue a new set of rules to end it. Wilensky, now a private lawyer in Minneapolis, has published a detailed blueprint for closing the loophole. The question is whether the new president will follow it.

For many of those on the right and left who have lamented the continuing power of Wall Street, "reinstate the Glass-Steagall Act" has been a rallying cry for reform. But that Depression-era law, which forced financial institutions to separate investment banking from depository banking and was repealed by President Bill Clinton and a Republican Congress in 1999, is as much a symbol as a solution. The financial collapse of 2008 happened not only because the firewall of Glass-Steagall was missing but also because regulators failed to police lax mortgage lenders and the banks that bundled and securitized mortgages many times over.

Elizabeth Warren, before she became a U.S. senator, chaired the commission that oversaw the Troubled Asset Relief Program (TARP) bailouts that immediately followed the housing crisis, and then served as an adviser to the Treasury Department, where she conceived of and helped launch the Consumer Financial Protection Bureau. Warren also favors a new Glass-Steagall law and has introduced one in the Senate. But more than that, she has identified very specific rule changes that transcend the symbolic and get to the heart of how Wall Street operates.

If you want to stop paying rents, know who exactly is collecting them. If the game is rigged, don't say so generally; say so precisely. And show precisely how to unrig it.

The pioneer of this method was Louis Brandeis, "the people's attorney," who more than a century ago represented oppressed garment workers in lawsuits demanding better working conditions and wages. He invented a method of painstaking investigation in reports that became known as "Brandeis briefs." The key to these briefs, which judges allowed even though they were not strictly about legal interpretation, was that they were forensic in their factual detail and (by the standards of the time) scientific in their narratives of causation: *because of a certain rule or its absence, the health and safety of the plaintiffs are threatened in the following concrete ways.*

Today this method is commonplace in public-interest law. But at the turn of the twentieth century, the very idea of public-interest law was still nascent. Brandeis would later serve on the U.S. Supreme Court. His innovation would become the template for the decisive briefs in cases such as *Brown v. Board of Education* in 1954, when NAACP lawyer Thurgood Marshall enlisted child-development experts to demonstrate, specifically and scientifically, that racial segregation harmed black children and that "separate but equal" was a contradiction in terms—a rule-set structured specifically to protect white power and to isolate black communities.

Chances are, you're not a public-interest lawyer or a social scientist. But you can still create a layperson's equivalent of a Brandeis brief on whatever causes you are championing. You can expose rent-seeking rules by bringing them and their consequences into the light of day.

LET SUNSHINE DISINFECT

It's not always the case that disclosure and transparency help level the playing field for everyday citizens. Consider campaign finance, where even limited rules for public disclosure of political contributions have created such a glut of "open" data about who gave how much to whom and when that most citizens stop paying attention altogether.

But in general, game-riggers prefer to operate out of view. Consider the problem of campus sexual assault. It used to be that most survivors kept their traumatic experience to themselves and suffered in isolation (while still having to share a library or classroom or dorm with their rapists or attackers). Even today, only 12 percent of student survivors report an assault to the police. There are many reasons for this, including fear of retaliation and peer pressure. But high among them is a sense that the university process for justice is at best opaque and at worst hostile to survivors.

Which is why two such survivors, Alexandra Brodsky and Dana Bolger, created Know Your IX, an organization to educate victims about the particulars: their legal protections under Title IX of the U.S. Education Amendments of 1972; the specific steps a victim can, cannot, or *must* take to secure those protections; exactly how and whether to file a complaint or a lawsuit (with templates); the common ways that colleges often mishandle or distort investigations to favor the accused; the tactics for mobilizing student voices or alumni dollars or media attention to force administrators to reform their policies.

Know Your IX started as a one-stop information website. It's now a network that organizes nationwide boot camps and teach-ins and prompted the White House to organize a task force on the issue of gender-based violence. By being so concrete about where and how victims and their advocates should apply pressure on the system, it is changing the norms, codes, and narratives around sexual assault.

Game-riggers rely on concealment and stealth. Re-riggers probe relentlessly. In Chicago, a public radio program on WBEZ called Curious City takes listener questions and turns them into well-reported on-air stories. One citizen named Janice Thomson recently asked: Where does Chicago get its electricity? She asked because voters in 2012 had passed a "municipal aggregation" referendum allowing the city to bulk-purchase electricity at lower rates for participating customers. She'd voted for it because it was touted as delivering "100 percent clean energy." But when WBEZ investigated, it found and reported that in fact a significant portion of the city's power came from fracking and natural gas rather than renewables like wind or solar.

As she recounts in her blog, Thomson then took three steps. She personally opted out of the "municipal aggregation" system and instead signed up for electricity from an Illinois wind farm.

She began taking courses from the Chicago Conservation Corps, on energy and environmental stewardship. And in partnership with C3, she launched a nonprofit campaign called Electric Community to teach citizens how to "green the grid." By asking a simple question about systems and engaging WBEZ, Thomson uncovered a rigged system, challenged it, and bypassed it.

Probing the rule book for weaknesses or ambiguities, asking why certain rules are structured the way they are, exploring who benefits from that structure, and revealing what you find: these require not expertise but its opposite. They require a nearly child-like imagination, an open-minded innocence about *why* the rules are what they are and an uncynical willingness to ask *what if* the rules changed.

Then, of course, they require doggedness: the doggedness to understand (or enlist others who can translate) the deliberately baroque or opaque ways that rules get rigged, and the doggedness to shine light relentlessly on the riggers. This is a regathering of the power we already have as everyday citizens. And it's a way to change the game.

STRATEGY 3: ATTACK YOUR OPPONENT'S PLAN

If power concentrates, and tends toward monopoly and winner-take-all politics, then you must change the game. The third strategy for doing that is attacking the opponent's plan (rather than his or her forces). Don't try to beat your adversaries at their own game. Paralyze, bypass, and undermine their strategy instead.

OODLES OF OODA: PARALYZE

Military metaphors are sometimes overused in discussions of political strategy. But there is a time when such metaphors are completely fitting: when you have to fight.

In the study and practice of warfare, the dominant approach is attrition: grind down the opposition's strongholds with overwhelming fire and force. When you have greater power and are contending with people who have less, attrition is your go-to strategy.

But this book is written for the power have-nots (or rather, for those people whose power is latent, rather than in full use already). And for you, attrition is generally not the answer. Maneuvering is. Maneuver warfare, in layman's terms, means relying on mobility, surprise, and combined forces to defeat the opposition. Or, as the United States Marine Corps puts it: "to shatter the enemy's cohesion through a variety of rapid, focused, and unexpected actions which create a turbulent and rapidly deteriorating situation with which the enemy cannot cope."

The U.S. Marines, a mobile expeditionary force designed to take on larger foes, have put maneuver warfare at the heart of their method. Their book of doctrine, *Warfighting,* explains that although attrition and maneuver may overlap in practice, the core theoretical differences between them dictate very different tactics. Attrition requires planned efficiency and centralization, approaches problems frontally, and measures success by destruction of the enemy's men and materiel. Maneuver requires speedy judgment and decentralization, circumvents problems, and measures success by disruption of the enemy's mindset and morale.

The Marine Corps was influenced strongly by the theoretical work of a former fighter pilot named John Boyd. After Vietnam, Boyd studied methods of maneuver from Sun Tzu's China to Hannibal at Cannae, from Grant at Vicksburg to Rommel's blitzkrieg and Sharon's attack across the Suez Canal. And he distilled the methods down to a single cycle that he called the "OODA loop." Conflict, Boyd said, is a continuous loop of *observation*, *orientation*, *decision*, and *action*. You observe the opponent. You orient yourself to the terrain. You decide how to move based on that orientation. You act. At that point, circumstances change and you start again.

The more rapidly you can move through this cycle, the more likely you are to gain an edge on your adversary. And that initial edge compounds as the conflict unfolds, building with each OODA loop, until the adversary loses cohesion and either panics or collapses. "Boyd-cycle" the enemy and you win. Throughout, you are seeking to redirect the other side's energy and force rather than confront it head-on. This is true whether you are a pilot in a dogfight, an infantry commander in a land skirmish—or an activist mobilizing citizens against an entrenched or superior power.

Maneuver is more than simple evasiveness or nimbleness. It is an approach to conflict in which you attack not the forces but the strategy of your adversary.

The ongoing fight against electronic surveillance by the NSA is a living case study of civic conflict by maneuver. Whatever you may think of Edward Snowden (hero, traitor, both?), there is no question that he and WikiLeaks, and eventually mainstream media outlets and some national politicians, were able to upend a consensus around this issue that had been silently skewed against common citizens. Intelligence agencies and national security elites were forced out of their default posture of omniscience and intimidation. They had to respond to disclosures they could neither control nor predict, and they had to justify openly what they had grown accustomed to compelling secretly.

Another and perhaps more visible example of maneuver in action is the push to raise the minimum wage to $15. Labor unions and liberals have been trying for years to raise the minimum wage. Business groups and conservatives have been trying for years to block or limit such raises. During all these years—decades, really—the two sides have been engaged in something like attrition warfare. Labor was definitely not winning.

The business case against a minimum-wage hike—indeed, against the minimum wage itself—had always been that it would raise costs and force employers to lay off workers. The strategy was simple intimidation ("It'd be a shame if you forced me to pay you more"), coupled with abstract but skillful zero-sum arguments about "wages versus jobs" that magically removed from consideration the idea of trimming corporate profits or executive pay.

Even though there was little compelling evidence for the idea that higher wages meant less employment, unions did not contest the argument so much as try to argue from fairness that workers deserved better. This was a weak position. It let stand the corporate assertion that "you can either have a job or you can have fairness."

And so Mary Kay Henry, head of the Service Employees International Union, decided to challenge this assumption. In late 2012, SEIU coordinated a series of surprise strikes by fast-food workers nationwide, to draw attention to their low wages and powerless work circumstances. #FastFoodForward became a phenomenon on social media, and its demands were soon boiled down to "$15 and a union." These were the first strikes by fast-food workers in living memory. They bloomed across the country. The press amplified them in every city. Strikes continued into the next year, putting fast-food companies on the defensive.

The $15 goal was concrete (rather than just a general call for a raise), non-random (roughly what the minimum wage would be today if it had kept pace with decades of gains in worker productivity), and audacious enough (at a time when the federal minimum was $7.25) to motivate workers.

No one pretended that $15 would cure inequality. But when opponents argued that $15 was "too high" for fast-food workers, they had stepped into terrain that had been chosen by SEIU: anyone could take a moment to imagine what it'd be like to live on even $15 an hour, much less a lower amount. Low wages were no longer an abstraction. And now the debate was about *what amount* would constitute a livable wage in America, rather than whether to have one at all.

David Rolf of SEIU then set the terms for the next phase of the fight. The leader of a home-care workers local in Seattle and one of Henry's leading lieutenants, Rolf decided to focus on the nearby town of Sea-Tac, where the region's airport is located. Working with community leaders and activists, Rolf and his team put a measure on the local ballot in 2013 proposing to raise the wage for airport and hospitality workers to $15.

Sea-Tac was a perfect arena. Filled with striving immigrants and low-wage baggage handlers, rental-car dispatchers, garage employees, skycaps, and other service workers, it was a place where people believed in hard work—but also the need for a better deal. And it was a small enough community so that only a few thousand votes would be sufficient for Proposition 1 to win—which it did, over the concerted resistance of major airlines, hotels, and restaurant chains.

One of the keys to victory was that the $15 advocates made their case on the basis not only of fairness but also prosperity. They made a "middle-out economics" argument—that when workers have more money in their pockets, they can buy more from local businesses, which then can afford to hire more workers, which sets in motion a positive feedback loop of increasing demand. This argument, that raising the wage is *good* for prosperity and jobs, worked. It overcame the classic fearmongering about layoffs. Labor won in Sea-Tac by attacking business's *strategy* of intimidation.

This was the first time in America that a municipality had enacted a $15 minimum wage. Now, using the same arguments, labor moved to unleash the next OODA cycle in Seattle. As the campaign for Proposition 1 had unfolded, Seattle was electing a new mayor and several council members. An avowed Socialist, Kshama Sawant, made $15 a rallying cry for her City Council campaign. Both mayoral candidates felt pressured to endorse $15 as well. Sawant ended up unseating a longtime councilmember. And Ed Murray, who became mayor, agreed within weeks of his election to create a task force of business, labor, and civic leaders to map out a pathway to $15 in Seattle.

I served on that task force, along with Rolf, Sawant, and others, including my middle-out-economics collaborator, Nick

Hanauer, a venture capitalist whose "strange-bedfellows" support for $15 had been crucial. As the closed-door negotiations unfolded, Sawant's avid followers and local unions applied continued pressure from the outside in public rallies and well-crafted media events.

A divided business community, feeling the heat from customers and the media, was unable to hold a united front in opposition. The default strategies of predicting economic doom for the region or threatening job losses or belittling the idea of service workers making $15 no longer worked. Business had been outmaneuvered.

A few months later, the task force announced a deal. Its details included a several-year phase-in and concessions to smaller employers. But the headlines the next day focused not on those details but on a simple and remarkable fact: in just a few months, one of the country's largest and most economically vibrant cities had just signed up for $15.

Seattle and Sea-Tac may have been uniquely primed to be the first victories, as Rolf recounts in his book, *The Fight for Fifteen*. But the core elements of maneuver as practiced by the Marine Corps—and the emphasis on neutralizing the opponent's strategy—are wholly transferable to other communities around the country.

And each turn of the OODA cycle makes the next one easier. Comparable coalitions have now secured victories to raise the wage in such cities as San Francisco and Louisville and Kansas City and Santa Fe, and states such as Nebraska and South Dakota and Oregon. A contagion of worker power has broken out across red and blue territory.

BRINGING BALLOTS TO A GUNFIGHT: BYPASS

Margaret Mead's famous statement about social change ("Never doubt that a small group of thoughtful, committed citizens can change the world. Indeed, it's the only thing that ever has") reminds us that big always starts small. But smalls create big change only when they can turn the status quo against itself.

Days after the massacre at Sandy Hook Elementary School, an Indiana mom named Shannon Watts went on Facebook and started venting. Other outraged mothers joined in. Their conversations bloomed into Moms Demand Action for Gun Sense in America, now a massive national grassroots network. At that same time, a small group of friends and I founded an organization in Washington State that became known as the Alliance for Gun Responsibility. When we started, we had no clear plan except to *do something* in our state—to show, despite the paralysis of Congress, that reform was possible.

The Alliance has since become a national pacesetter because it has organized and won two statewide ballot initiatives—the first one, to create a system of universal background checks for gun purchases; the second, to create "extreme risk protection orders" that keep firearms out of the hands of those who pose a grave danger to themselves or others. In each campaign the goal was clear: to win. But winning those campaigns, arduous and exhilarating to be sure, was in service of a greater goal.

As its full name suggests, the Alliance exists to reduce gun violence by promoting gun *responsibility* as a needed counterweight to gun *rights*. Every effort of the Alliance is about resetting that normative, cultural, and political balance: creating a society where

Second Amendment absolutism is understood as irresponsible, and where gun policy follows such a balanced sensibility. We respect the right to bear arms. We also believe that only toddlers and sociopaths try to claim rights without responsibilities.

The clarity of that position makes the Alliance something other than a "gun control" group. Its goal is culture change—the acceptance, by gun *owners* themselves, of a public-minded ethic of responsibility. This focus enables the Alliance to mobilize all forms of citizen power, from money (some of the state's wealthiest citizens have been major backers) to people (moms, survivors of gun violence, and many gun owners) to social norms (by working with public-health practitioners to promote an ethic of gun responsibility) with a distinctive sense of purpose.

In this work we are in direct conflict with the National Rifle Association and the gun lobby generally. But that does not mean our method is direct conflict. Instead, we have been bypassing their strengths and exposing their limitations. More to the point, we have been attacking their strategy.

The approach of the NRA leadership has grown more uncompromising and even radical over the years, making it less broadly appealing but, in these polarized times, more politically potent. And their strategy has been to own legislatures. They threaten to rain negative ads and angry voters on any legislator in a nonliberal district who might be tempted to stray from their agenda. Their reputation for retribution, even more than actual dollars or voters mobilized, enables them to scare legislators into submission.

The Alliance initially tried to get the Washington legislature, in the session that opened just weeks after Sandy Hook, to enact universal background checks. The NRA cowed enough members—

Democrats as well as Republicans—to kill the bill. We lost when we played the game on their terms.

But polls consistently show that majorities of the general public and citizens of both parties support the measures that the Alliance advocates, as do most NRA *members*. So after our defeat in the state capitol, the Alliance immediately pivoted. We converted the bill that had died in the legislature into a ballot initiative. We went straight to the people, gathering hundreds of thousands of signatures and raising millions of dollars for the campaign. Eleven months after Sandy Hook, we won with over 60 percent of the statewide vote. It was the first time in the country that background checks had been enacted by a vote of the people.

That laid the foundation for our next victory in 2016, a ballot initiative on extreme risk protection orders. More than that, however, it opened up a new strategy. Coordinating with activists in other states and cities with direct democracy, we are working to seed gun-responsibility ballot measures across the country— and to force the NRA into a wide-open game of Whac-A-Mole. Now, in multiple jurisdictions at once, the gun lobby has to argue against common-sense measures before an entire electorate and not just a handful of captured legislators. That's an expensive, sprawling proposition. And it will expose the fact that the NRA has less money than people think, less capacity to play outside of controlled state capitals, and less command over its own membership.

Because the NRA and the gun manufacturers who bankroll it are savvy, they will surely adapt. And they will likely own Congress for a very long time, because ballot initiatives exist only at the state level, not nationally. But the experience of the

Alliance reminds us that even a dominant power is only as strong as its strategy.

GUERRILLA CITIZENSHIP: UNDERMINE

All around the world are people with few visible forms of power at their disposal who manage to shape their societies passively. In *Weapons of the Weak*, his incisive 1985 study of the Malay peasantry, James Scott describes the many subtle ways that poor peasant farmers engaged in "everyday forms of resistance." Foot-dragging, willful misunderstanding of mandates from landlords and officials, ritualized performances of defiance, outright sabotage—all have been part of an unstated, unending re-litigation of the social contract in Malaysia.

Power from below also can arise from unplanned collective action. In his insightful book *Life as Politics*, Asef Bayat describes "social nonmovements—uncoordinated choices to practice a way of everyday life" that may not evolve into formal political action but that nonetheless change the frame of the politically possible. In Iran, for instance, young people have chosen to adopt styles of *fun*—in clothing, music, food, books, gender mixing, and slang—that subtly defy official Islamist culture. Those young people, like the daring youth who wore blue jeans in Soviet-era Moscow, are making choices of resistance. Their choices are not organized by anyone in particular but they are tacitly connected in a quiet form of dissent that generates power from below.

That kind of intuitive, uncoordinated resistance from below may be necessary in a society with a sharply unequal power

structure. It is often one of the few ways that people who are oppressed can express their frustration or show any agency. But as a
method of social change, it is always insufficient. Movements that
truly change a society will cohere only when *intuitive* and *uncoordinated* activity becomes *intentional* and *well-coordinated*. Only
when the disenfranchised become organized and directed toward
actively unmaking the system do they become capable of true
revolution.

Mao Zedong, in his long war to take control of China in the
1930s and 1940s, took a most cold-eyed inventory of his situation.
He knew his Communist forces did not have the advantage in
trained soldiers or materiel or diplomatic alliances; the rival Nationalists, backed by the United States, had that edge (and their
common enemy, the Japanese, had the most powerful military
in Asia). He knew as well that he could not rally a sympathetic
urban proletariat, as the Leninist playbook prescribed: China's
cities were not industrialized enough and were in many cases
controlled by the Nationalists. What Mao did have were millions
of beleaguered peasants primed for change, his own knowledge
of the rural and remote areas of the country—and the option to
buy time.

So he shaped his approach accordingly, by relying extensively
on such insurgent tactics and strategic retreats as the Long March,
and by investing heavily in propaganda and mass political education as he moved through the countryside. He let the Nationalists
bear the brunt of fighting against the Japanese Army, even as he
undermined the Nationalists with guerrilla warfare.

By the time military circumstances had shifted in his favor—
the end of World War II found the Nationalist forces depleted—he

was able to pivot to a more direct strategy of frontal assault with regular military forces. The Communists took over the mainland in 1949, forcing the Nationalists to flee to Taiwan. But Mao had won much earlier when he internalized one of Sun Tzu's core dictums from *The Art of War*: "What is of supreme importance in war is to attack the enemy's strategy."

When Nelson Mandela was a young firebrand in the African National Congress, he studied Mao closely. He also studied other rebellions and revolutionary movements, from Menachem Begin in Israel to the Boers (the descendants of his Afrikaner enemy) in the Anglo-Boer War. Of course he also studied Gandhi and *satyagraha*, the doctrine of nonviolent resistance that the ANC from the outset had adopted. What Mandela came to believe, though, was that nonviolence was not a moral requirement. It was only a tactical option—one that wasn't working. So he convinced the ANC to allow him to form a force for armed resistance to apartheid and the Afrikaner regime in South Africa.

In his memoir *Long Walk to Freedom*, Mandela justified this stance thus: "Non-violent passive resistance is effective as long as your opposition adheres to the same rules as you do. But if peaceful protest is met with violence, its efficacy is at its end."

Mandela did not have long to practice violent resistance before he was brought to trial for acts of sabotage. And here is the irony: it was the decades-long imprisonment that followed—not his choice to embrace violence—that gave Mandela the moral standing and power to negotiate apartheid's end. Mandela the firebrand tried to play the Afrikaner game of violence. Mandela the inmate—who transcended his hatred, who humanized his captors, who carried himself with a self-control and dignity that shamed those captors—was forced by circumstance to reinvent "peaceful protest" and to be reminded of its efficacy.

This was guerrilla warfare of a different kind. It did not involve blowing up train stations or ambushing army patrols. What he did on Robben Island was to undermine the Afrikaner regime with a most passive form of moral aggression.

Right here and right now in the United States, it is possible to practice what we might call "guerrilla citizenship"—organizing other people to act in a way that disrupts the plans and methods of the dominant power.

Remember the religious leaders in Missouri advocating for a "moral economy" and an end to usurious payday lending? In 2014, over a hundred of them went to the state capitol to protest the Missouri Senate's refusal to accept Obamacare's Medicaid expansion. They came with a simple question: "Does this measure threaten or enhance the dignity of everyday Missourians?" Unable to secure meetings with legislative leaders, they went to the Senate gallery to pray and sing together on behalf of the poor and vulnerable whose health and lives were being held hostage to partisan politics.

Twenty-three of them were arrested, most from Kansas City and twenty-one of them African American. Worse, vindictive politicians ensured that the charges would not be dropped. So two years later, this group of urban clergy and faith leaders stood trial and was convicted of trespassing—the only crime their peaceful protests could be said to have constituted—by a predominantly white jury from the middle of the state. There had not been a case like this since 1967, when a largely African American group of clergy was tried for assembling on the steps of the capitol in South Carolina. The #Medicaid23 became famous. The verdict did not silence them; it made them louder.

Their case echoes the work of the Moral Mondays movement, a weekly grassroots protest that started in North Carolina, when the legislature in 2014 enacted restrictions on voting rights. The Moral Mondays movement, catalyzed initially by faith leaders such as Reverend William Barber and then expanding to a broad coalition of progressive citizen activists, has since spread to Georgia, South Carolina, Illinois, and several other states. Thus far it has not forced any legislature to make a dramatic policy change. But the movement derives its power from its continuous presence. Each week, citizens meet at the capitol in Raleigh, protest, get arrested, and return in seven days for more. They are not just bearing witness. By refusing to leave or to quit the capitol, they are using the omnipresence of the legislature against itself.

And guerrilla citizenship doesn't even have to involve a real-life conflict. The libertarian author Charles Murray argues in his book *By the People* that the only way to unwind the corrupt, overreaching administrative machinery of the federal government is for citizens to engage in mass civil disobedience against laws and rules. He proposes the creation by private philanthropists of something called the Madison Fund, to finance the cost of the litigation and penalties that would ensue.

It's a radical, provocative idea. And though it hasn't been implemented, the very notion of citizens collectively choosing to disobey and disregard regulations en masse, while also accepting that the rule of law means taking the punishment, is an imaginative way of undermining the power of the state. If anyone ever takes up Murray on his idea—and it may not be from the right, or on the issues he cares about most—it will be a reminder to us all:

Many smalls can always overwhelm the big—if we get activated.

CHANGE THE STORY

STRATEGY 4: DESCRIBE THE ALTERNATIVE

Now we proceed to the next three strategies, which all fall under the imperative of changing the story. Recall: *If power creates a story of why it's legitimate, then you must change the story.* The first strategy for doing that is to describe an alternative allocation of power and an alternative basis for legitimacy. You can't beat something with nothing. You have to expand the public's sense of what's possible—by asking provocative and audacious *what if* questions; by describing a better way in detail; and by offering a new values-based definition of what ought to be considered "normal."

WHAT IF

One of Gloria Steinem's techniques, honed over decades of activism, is simple reversal. When presented with a frame of thought or judgment that implicitly assigns privilege to men or disadvantage to women, she asks what it would look like if the gender roles were reversed.

Steinem started this in the 1970s with an essay called "If Men Could Menstruate" (she imagines at length how men would celebrate menstruation, make it the center of a manhood ritual, honor it in public spaces, and favor it in federal policy). She goes on to ask: What if Sigmund Freud had been born Phyllis Freud? How would our cultural notions of penis envy collapse if they'd been framed as womb envy?

Reversal became one of her most reliable rhetorical devices. But it was more than that. It was a habit—of imagination and self-assertion. She has made it a routine for so many activists—men as well as women—to ask *what if* so that they can, in her words, "uncover the distance between *what is* and *what could be*." Through her books and unending stream of lectures, Steinem has inscribed this routine, so simple and repeatable, into the playbooks of innumerable other feminists.

The Bechdel-Wallace test is a similarly simple device, created by the cartoonist Alison Bechdel and her friend Liz Wallace, for evaluating whether movies and television shows perpetuate gender inequity. *Does a film have at least two named women in it, talking to each other, about something other than a man?* A depressingly large number of films and shows fail the test. But it does more than scold. It suggests an alternate reality—an achievable one—in which women have an equal presence in mass popular culture, and the screen represents more than just the gaze of a (non-feminist) man.

The social media surge in 2015 around #OscarsSoWhite, which highlighted the absence of nonwhite nominees for major Academy Awards, has jolted Hollywood into greater self-awareness of its own lack of diversity. It's prompted the Academy of Motion Picture Arts and Sciences to add more people of color into the pool of Oscar voters. And it has opened a wider debate about casting, auditioning, and the conduits of power that bring movies to the screen. Like the Bechdel-Wallace test, #OscarsSoWhite exposed inequities that many people had stopped noticing or had never even seen.

The same can—and must—be said of Black Lives Matter, both the hashtag and the loosely networked activist movement that has arisen out of it.

The phrase "Black Lives Matter" has become controversial for reasons that reveal the power illiteracy and selective deafness of its critics. That becomes clear if we imagine the pregnant silences around and between those three words. Listen for them: Black lives matter *finally*. Black lives *also* matter. Black lives *shouldn't* matter *less*. The activists are implying those unspoken words, even if their opponents do not hear them.

This is the central imaginative and strategic move of Black Lives Matter. To say the phrase is to ask, in effect, *What if* black lives mattered? *What if* they mattered as much to our society, government, and institutions as white lives always have? Which forces us all to face the history, legacy, and persistence of white supremacy in law and culture. Choose your metric: life expectancy, quality of schooling, housing discrimination, job discrimination, health outcomes, wealth, income, criminalization, execution. On every measure, America truly values black life less highly than white (indeed, non-black) life.

In this light, "all lives matter" is not, as its exponents intend, a rebuttal to "black lives matter." It is confirmation of it. If all lives truly mattered, it would not be necessary to say "black lives matter." Yet it is. The willful blindness that prevents so many Americans from understanding this—that treats any black or brown plea for equal treatment as a plea for *preferential* treatment—is a symptom of mass delusion.

Black Lives Matter, then, is an overdue, indispensable wake-up call. What's needed after any wake-up call, however, is a concrete call to action.

A BETTER WAY

Let's consider in more depth the issue of policing and police shootings of brown and black civilians, the issue that has given rise to Black Lives Matter. One of the most potentially transformative calls to action to have emerged in response is called Campaign Zero. It is a detailed policy agenda and organizing platform for reducing the number of police killings in the United States. Not to a more manageable or reasonable level. To *zero*. To appreciate how dramatic a shift that would be, consider that more than 1,000 people are killed by police every year. Sixty percent of them were unarmed or were in situations that did not require violent intervention.

Campaign Zero was organized by four young activists who have been on the front lines of protest yet also have enough savvy and experience to convert protest into durable power: Brittany Packnett, the head of Teach for America in St. Louis and an activist who served on the Ferguson Commission and on President Obama's police reform commission; St. Louis community organizer Johnetta Elzie; Samuel Sinyangwe, a data scientist; and the activist DeRay Mckesson.

Together they have laid out a body of work that includes ten categories of policy and practice reform, a bevy of supporting research documents, a transparent tool showing how they have revised the platform in response to feedback and critique, and tools for organizing other people to support the platform. Their statement of intention is direct:

"We can end police violence in America." It then elaborates: "We can live in an America where the police do not kill people. Police in England, Germany, Australia, Japan, and even cities like Buffalo, NY, and Richmond, CA, demonstrate that public safety can be ensured without killing civilians. By implementing the right policy changes, we can end police killings and other forms of police violence in the United States."

The dominant narrative in American civic life, promoted by many in today's police and political establishment, says that some police violence is the necessary price for law and order. Campaign Zero lays out an alternative that doesn't just challenge the dominant, self-justifying narrative; it displaces it altogether. *We can believe in zero.*

If you want to change the story that justifies current structures of power and privilege, you must have such a combination of bold goals and specific steps. Marc Freedman, on a very different issue, has applied this lesson to great effect. Freedman is founder of Encore.org, an organization working to redefine retirement in America.

Most Americans have a "golden years" ideal of retirement as a time of leisure, travel, and self-indulgent consumerism. But as Freedman points out, this vision was invented (mainly by corporations), and it can be reinvented (mainly by citizens). Baby boomers are living longer and working longer as well. This is a generation that wants something more purposeful than endless golf. So in the midst of this longevity revolution and quest for meaning, Freedman has boldly strived to rebrand the second half of life as an "encore career"—a time to deploy all one's life experience in new work for the greater good.

He's written books that make the case for this new vision of aging. He's partnered with media entities of every kind to spread the Encore gospel. But most important, he and his team have built a national infrastructure of programs and activities to give life to the vision. He created the Purpose Prize, which awards grants of up to $100,000 to Americans over sixty doing great civic and pro-social work in their encore careers. He created Encore Fellowships, to place a network of older private-sector workers in local nonprofits as they transition into an encore career. He has worked with AARP, major foundations, and university continuing-education programs to popularize this new narrative of midlife and beyond as a time of learning, engagement, and service.

When you look at any of the winners of the Purpose Prize (for which I have been a judge) or the Encore Fellows, you see not just inspiring individuals; you see a better way to age. *They* are happier. People like Belle Mickelson, a science teacher and amateur bluegrass fiddler who decided upon retiring to start a traveling music camp that serves Native youth in small villages across Alaska and uses the music as a way to promote suicide prevention. People like Laura Safer Espinoza, a former judge in New York who set out to retire in sunny Florida—and ended up becoming, in her encore, an advocate for the tomato pickers of Immokalee. You see in such people a vibrant, other-directed alternative to the default image of retirement as complacent senescence.

For all the traction that Encore.org has gotten in just over a decade, this movement is not about to obliterate the structure of market and government incentives and norms that promote the old way of imagining retirement. But it's on the right track. Freedman started out in the early 1990s launching Experience Corps, a program inspired by the late John Gardner that enlisted older adults to volunteer as literacy tutors for struggling students. So the idea of creating multigenerational compacts is core to his operating style. But what he's learned in his experience as the "encore career" proselytizer is that before you activate people with programs, you awaken them with a new story of purpose. There is untold power in that yearning.

NEW NORMALS

The idea of a universal basic income (UBI)—a guaranteed minimum that every citizen would receive—has been in circulation for decades. One early and prominent advocate was the free-market economist Milton Friedman, who saw it as a way to replace welfare and encouraged President Nixon to propose it (as a "negative income tax"). More recently some progressives, most prominently former union leader Andy Stern, have come out strongly in favor as well, arguing that it creates a wage floor for low-income workers.

In June 2016, a Swiss referendum to create a universal basic income—a grant of the equivalent of about $2,500 for every adult and $650 for every child in Switzerland—was soundly defeated. But to the activists behind the measure, that loss was a win. Why? Because it put the idea, once considered fringe or utterly utopian, on the mainstream agenda.

It sparked a national debate about how a UBI could be used to combat inequality. It set the stage for a possible follow-up referendum. And polls showed that it began to create a creeping sense of inevitability about a UBI—a plurality of Swiss citizens expected the country would have one within five years.

In the United States, meanwhile, some reform conservatives and tech-minded liberals are coming together to discuss and propose a UBI here. The picture they paint is of a society where robots and globalization make many of today's jobs obsolete. A UBI, in their view, does more than establish a baseline for dignity and economic security; it frees all people, and not just the very privileged, to pursue their passions and talents. It converts the creative destruction of automated capitalism into a creative opportunity.

We are a long way from that vision or a UBI. But the emerging buzz around it forces us to imagine what is currently unimaginable in a country where half of new jobs are low-wage but not living-wage: a future of *guaranteed economic security*. It also highlights one of the most important parts of changing what people think is politically possible: you must describe, on the level of *values*, what a new normal could be.

Ai-jen Poo is a civic catalyst who, like Marc Freedman, thinks and acts intergenerationally. Poo is the founder of the National Domestic Workers Alliance. For years she has organized caregivers, nannies, and other domestic workers, a workforce of mainly immigrant women who were isolated, household by household, and often subject to abuse, wage theft, and mistreatment by their employers.

Poo brought them out of isolation. She helped them find their voice together. She helped them learn how to lobby lawmakers, how to advocate for reform, how to tell their own stories in public. The NDWA pushed several states to enact a Domestic Workers' Bill of Rights and is still pushing Congress to amend laws, born of the Old South, that exempt domestic workers from many of the labor protections that other workers enjoy.

In all this work, Poo and her colleagues are very conscious of the power of story—and the need to change the story of power. When the film *The Help* was released, the NDWA collaborated with the studio to open up wider conversations about injustices in domestic work past and present. The organization has created similar ventures with other pop-culture makers in film, television, and sports.

But perhaps the most intriguing work Poo is doing has transcended her own organization. She is focused on the demographic "silver tsunami" now transforming America: the aging boom driven by the life cycle of the largely white Baby Boom. What she has also realized, though, is that the people who will be caring for that aging population are largely nonwhite. This could portend an epic clash of generations and cultures. Poo envisions it instead as a chance to bridge them.

So she has launched a campaign called Caring Across Generations, whose purpose is to foster a culture of care in the United States. To be sure, that means making systemic policy reforms in long-term care and home care. More fundamentally, though, it means sparking an ethical revolution.

A caring society values grandparents and other elders. A caring society treats caregiving not as a commodity or cost to be minimized but as a gift to be honored and valued. A caring society seeks to support deep, cross-cultural relationships between those who need care and those who provide it. A caring society supports the families of those who need care. A caring society treats the ethic of care not as a soft nice-to-have in a harsh Darwinian world but as the vital must-have that enables a society to thrive.

If we in the United States were to establish care in this way as a central norm, not just in words but in deeds, and not just in private but in public, then changes in our institutions and policy frameworks would follow. Legal and economic arrangements would magically move, like iron filings pulled across a tray by an unseen magnet beneath.

In our country, there is so much that's wrong with the way we deliver care to the aging, the very young, and the infirm. But you can't beat something with nothing. It is not enough to decry what's broken. You have to describe the alternative and make it possible for people to believe in it. To care.

STRATEGY 5: ORGANIZE IN NARRATIVES

If power creates a story of why it's legitimate, then you must change the story. Our next strategy for doing that is organizing in narratives. That is, using story to organize people and then allowing people to organize themselves into the story. Your narratives have to challenge the dominant story line of why things are the way they are. To do that, you have to stir up a new sense of "us"; provide an overarching explanation for who has what and why; and awaken the hero's spirit in every citizen.

WHO IS US?

Story teaches agency and empathy, child psychologists say: it teaches how to deduce cause and effect and imagine other people's minds. Story girds us for conflict, as any screenwriter worth his or her salt will tell you. Story gives pattern to the unknowable, as mythmakers ancient and contemporary know. It is the bonding agent in social cohesion. It is the catalytic agent for changing the status quo.

Marshall Ganz, one of the greatest community organizers alive, knows all this. He learned his art as a civil rights worker in Mississippi in the 1960s, then went on to organize migrant farmworkers with Cesar Chavez. He developed the organizing tools and strategies used by the first Obama presidential campaign, training trainers in what was called Camp Obama. He has mentored countless social-justice organizers around the planet. He teaches now at Harvard, where, twenty-eight years after dropping out, he returned to finish his degree and get a doctorate. He is the quintessential teacher-as-learner.

Everywhere he goes, Ganz uses a method for organizing that centers on three nested narratives: the story of *self*, the story of *us*, and the story of *now*.

He teaches organizers entering into any setting to start not with policy proposals or high concepts like justice but with biographies—their own, and those of the people they hope to mobilize. What are the stories you tell about yourself? Why do you tell them that way? How can we find connections across our stories of origin that build trust and common cause?

That work then flows into the story of *us*: the collective narratives of challenge, choice, and purpose that emerge from any community—that, in fact, help define it. This is how in a place like New Orleans after the flood or Detroit after the crash, residents can develop a shared identity of resilience and reinvention. It's how anti–Common Core activists nationwide have been able to forge a cross-ideological crusade of parents and teachers tired of standardized-testing regimes that crush creativity and stifle liberty.

Once that shared narrative is activated, the organizer can connect it to the fierce urgency of *now*—a story about why this is the "movement moment," when individual and collective motivations converge, and when action is needed and possible. Why this and no other time is the time for change. This is how "Yes We Can" became more than a slogan in 2008, as "Morning in America" did in 1980. Or "Make America Great Again" in 2016.

Of these three stories, the middle—about us—is crucial. Any effort to exercise citizen power depends on creating new answers to the question: Who is "us"?

During the campaign for a $15 minimum wage in Seattle, one of the most potent speeches I heard was from a woman named Evelyn, a sixty-something Filipina immigrant who cleans rooms at a Sea-Tac Airport hotel. Her husband is a baggage handler at the airport. It was a fund-raising event for the campaign, and this was her first public speech. And though she had never heard of Marshall Ganz before, in her short and blunt remarks she intuitively hit each of his marks. She talked about how a higher wage would enable her to catch up on her bills (*self*). She talked about why this was a unique opportunity to make gains for working people (*now*).

But she was at her most effective when she talked about what kind of Seattle we wanted to be, and why the city would be stronger if the people who do the thankless work could afford to live there, too. In short, she redefined *us*. She redrew the circles of identity, not as low-wage workers versus high-wage workers but as people who hold true Seattle values of inclusion versus those who don't.

This redrawing of the circles is also how "deep canvassing"— intensive face-to-face front-porch conversations based on personal storytelling—can change minds and win adherents on contentious issues like gay and transgender rights. Two young political scientists, Josh Kalla of Berkeley and David Broockman of Stanford, have conducted pioneering field experiments on deep canvassing.

One of the strategies that they found most effective was "analogic perspective taking," in which canvassers would invite citizens to talk about times when they had been treated unfairly for seeming "different." From there the canvasser could pivot to what those citizens had in common with gay or transgender people, and could often awaken enough empathy to reduce bias.

This is more than stepping into someone else's shoes. It's stepping into the story of how someone else came to be wearing those shoes.

If you are trying to convince your neighbors that a nearby church should be allowed to host a temporary homeless encampment, how do you deploy story? Maybe sometimes it will be by deriding the selfishness of those who resist. More often it will be by appealing to the better angels of all, so that even resisters can join without losing face. Either way, you are crafting an imagined *us* in order to create a real majority. In a town with excellent schools that attracts young families, how do you deal with the divide between the newcomers who are driving up property values and the old-timers who don't have school-age kids and want lower taxes? Again, you create a story of us—of common interest—that will either transcend that divide or sharpen it in a way that isolates the holdouts.

Such stories are weapons in an endless contest for legitimacy. The civil rights movement was (and is still) a decades-long argument about *Who is us.* The 2016 presidential election was a lurid referendum on the question. In this time of unprecedented economic inequality, the American self-story as a "middle-class nation" is eroding rapidly. The day when a majority of Americans are people of color is now within sight. Meanwhile, political polarization is at its highest since the Civil War. These are strong centrifugal forces. Who will legitimately get to speak for the United States during such a time? Who can embody and represent us?

That is not primarily a question about presidential candidates. It is a question about citizens, and what groups of us can best organize the imagination—and claim the "us."

POWER STORIES

Power justifies itself, in countless small ways. But one of the big ways it does so is by creating an ideological narrative about how things got to be this way—and what must now change. These narratives are more than technical explanations. They are epic morality tales, and they typically follow this sequence:

Paradise → Paradise Lost → Paradise Redeemed

They start with an ideal alignment of values and institutions that existed "once upon a time." They describe how that ideal was attacked from without and betrayed from within. Then they make clear that the only way people can get what they universally want—happiness and a fair shot—is to realign people, money, ideas, social norms, and other sources of power back to the old array. To fight and to challenge the status quo.

In 1971, the lawyer Lewis Powell sent a memorandum to the U.S. Chamber of Commerce. It detailed what he said was a concerted attack on the "free enterprise system" that was being channeled through television, magazines, universities, politicians, and celebrity crusaders such as Ralph Nader. He decried the growth of government and the spread of a mindset of dependency on government. He told a tale of liberal conspiracy, conservative complacency, and a slow-motion surrender by capitalists. Then he laid out a plan for counterattack: a methodical activation of money, ideas, people, politicians, and culture to elevate and enshrine "free enterprise" as a way of life and a legal regime.

Powell, who would go on to become a Supreme Court justice (as a Nixon nominee), is credited with catalyzing a generation-long effort on the right to bankroll think tanks, groom talent for the judiciary, create intellectual journals, and set up policy shops. The Cato Institute, the Heritage Foundation, the Federalist Society—these and many other conservative and libertarian powerhouses that gave force to the Reagan revolution grew out of this moment. Powell created the blueprint and his allies the infrastructure for what could, without prejudice, be called "the vast right-wing conspiracy." And he did so with story.

More than four decades later—decades during which the right was ascendant in national politics—the lawyer and political catalyst Rob Stein founded the Democracy Alliance, a network of mega-donors who coordinate investment in progressive political causes. When he was initially pitching the idea of the DA, he developed what became a famous PowerPoint presentation that showcased the Powell memo and its method, and he mirrored it: he told a story about *conservative* conspiracy and *liberal* complacency, about a left getting left behind and in urgent need of awakening.

Stein's story also worked. From that PowerPoint presentation and his impassioned pleas emerged what is now seen as the vital hub of a "vast left-wing conspiracy"—a progressive ecosystem of think tanks, leadership incubators, list-building technology, and other movement infrastructure.

Whether one side or the other is correct that it is "behind" and "under assault" is not the point. This is democratic politics—mobilization and countermobilization, in what is (in the best-case scenario) perpetual jostling for advantage, fueled by a perpetual sense of paranoia that one's opposition has attained insurmountable advantages.

What's notable in both cases is that the activists understood that a key to changing the story in national politics is organizing in story. Institutionalizing ideology. Across the political spectrum, story provides both the motivation and the ideological coherence for effective organizing—for power, and countervailing power.

And this instinct is not confined to the conservative-progressive, Republican-Democrat duopoly. In recent years, libertarians have been gaining followers, especially among millennials. Students for Liberty, the global network of campus libertarian organizations, has been expanding its reach significantly. They've done it by organizing with anti-war and anti–nanny state narratives about the true spirit of freedom, the evils of socialism (Bernie Sanders was a useful foil in 2016), the moral bankruptcy of the two-party system (Trump and Clinton were similarly useful), and the common-sense appeal of applying a tech-infused "à la carte" approach to politics.

In short, they've been telling a story about how these times don't just facilitate but *demand* a third option. The paradise they describe as having been lost—and now is ready to be redeemed— is a society with radically less government and collectivism than today's and radically more individualism and choice. That story can become self-fulfilling when it is used not only to intrigue or inspire but to mobilize and organize.

HEROES IN REAL LIFE

Of course, the dynamic at work here—that power is best orga-nized when it is organized by story—holds true in arenas far re-moved from partisan politics. Andrew Slack is an exuberant and kinetic young activist (and occasional comedian) steeped in popu-lar culture. He devoured the Harry Potter books when they came out. As he did, he realized that they had created more than a rabid base of readers and fans; they had created an untapped global net-work of potential activists.

So in 2005 he invented the Harry Potter Alliance, an orga-nization "to create heroes for the real world," as he put it. Using the story lines, characters, and moral quandaries from the novels, Slack invited young readers to identify with causes like combating genocide in Darfur, protecting LGBT rights, and welcoming un-documented immigrants ("What would Dumbledore do?").

He mobilized fans to give money, make media, pressure law-makers, donate books. He didn't seek permission from the series author J. K. Rowling or her publisher to create this endeavor in the name of their character. He just ran relentlessly with his epiphany. When Rowling soon discovered Slack's handiwork, she gave it her enthusiastic blessing and featured it on her own website. Lions-gate, which produced the Harry Potter films, initially told Slack to cease and desist, but when the fans organized a Change.org peti-tion on behalf of their alliance, the studio reversed course.

The Harry Potter Alliance now is a thriving nonprofit orga-nization with chapters around the world. It has activated millions of young people. It has applied its method to other pop-culture franchises, including the Hunger Games and Star Wars. And it has pioneered a form of fan activism that literally organizes power through story. It all began with Slack's insight into perhaps one of the most elemental facts of human nature and civic power: we all want to be the hero of our own tale. Those who can tap into that yearning win.

One of the HPA's most noteworthy recent campaigns was called "Superman Is an Immigrant." In fact, Superman was an *undocumented* immigrant. He was born on another planet, brought to our country without legal authorization when he was a baby, and raised here while hiding his true identity. No one recognized his great powers to do good. On Tumblr and Twitter and Facebook and Reddit, the HPA encouraged the undocumented immigrant activists known as the Dreamers, their allies, and other young people to spread this meme and to take selfies summarizing their own family's immigration story and how it connected to Superman's slogan of "Truth, Justice, and the American Way."

This brilliant campaign—an example of what Slack calls "cultural acupuncture"—grew out of a collaboration between the HPA and another story-minded organization called Define American. Define American exists on one level to promote better conversations about immigration policy and reform. On a deeper level, though, it exists to transform how this country sees people who are viewed as "illegal"—and to use story as a tool for challenging American cultural and civic conceptions of what a "real" American is.

Jose Antonio Vargas and Jake Brewer were two of Define American's prime founders. Vargas is a Pulitzer Prize–winning journalist and documentarian who grew up in suburban California; Brewer, a civic technology activist and policy wonk who grew up in rural Tennessee. Brewer came to consider Vargas "the gay, Filipino brother I never had." What sealed that bond was Vargas's decision in 2011 to come out as undocumented. He did so in a *New York Times Magazine* cover story, in which he confessed that he'd been brought to the country illegally as a child and that ever since high school, when he discovered his status, he'd kept it secret from all but a few friends.

Coming out was courageous, even heroic. It was also controversial. But Vargas knew that with his high profile and extensive media relationships, he was at far less risk of deportation than most of the young undocumented immigrants who until recently had felt they needed to hide their lie. So he decided to spend his capital on their behalf. Out of that moment, he and Brewer created an organization to re-humanize the call for immigration reform, help give voice to the 11 million undocumented—and challenge the default idea that an American is a native-born heartland white man like Brewer.

Define American harvests and distributes the stories of a wide range of Americans, including the young and undocumented, who now, like Vargas, have found that in coming out—and claiming their Americanness—they are newly powerful, even if newly exposed. They are no longer giving away their power to a system that criminalizes their very existence. Define American convinced Associated Press reporters and other journalists to stop using the label "illegal immigrants," on the notion that acts can be illegal but a *person* cannot. The organization sponsors film festivals and online campaigns and campus events to spread an idea of American identity based on contribution rather than birthright. Vargas is an itinerant preacher who goes not only to safe blue enclaves but also to Fox News and deep-red communities in the Deep South and Midwest. He relentlessly and compassionately engages critics and haters on social media.

There are many Americans who have the papers but don't live like citizens, and many who lack the papers but do. Vargas is a living reminder of this truth, and Brewer had unique standing to point it out to the rest of the country. But in 2015, Brewer died in a cycling accident while he was on a cancer-research charity ride. His death at age thirty-four made national news: he was at the time an aide to President Obama, but his wife, Mary Katherine Ham, was a prominent conservative commentator, and so the shock and grief touched circles and networks that don't often overlap.

For a brief moment, many on the left and right alike agreed that what had made Jake Brewer a great American was not the status and privilege he'd been born into by chance but the choices he'd made to *earn* his citizenship. Choices like regarding Jose Antonio Vargas as his brother. In death, Jake reminded many people that the dominant story line about "illegals" and "Americans" is outmoded, simplistic, and inhumane. Now it falls to Jose and others to extend that moment into a story-powered movement.

STRATEGY 6: MAKE YOUR FIGHT A FABLE

If power creates a story of why it's legitimate, then you must change the story. Our final strategy for doing this is to pick a fight that is emblematic, that can stand as a microcosm of the bigger moral and political stakes. In short, to turn a battle into a fable. This

means creating potent symbols for your cause, finding protago-
nists whose own story personifies the issue, and crystallizing it into
a single clear principle.

SYMBOLIZE

What converts an interested bystander into an active citizen?

The researcher Kate Krontiris recently led a fascinating research project for Google on this question. It focused on the nearly
50 percent of Americans who are aware of issues but who rarely
voice their opinions or take concrete action. (This is in contrast
to the 15 percent who are outright disengaged and the 35 percent
who are more actively engaged.) These interested bystanders,
Krontiris and her colleagues found, were most likely to get involved if they'd had prior personal experience on the issue, could
get emotional fulfillment from engaging, or believed their own
interests were at stake.

Narrative—especially narrative with symbolic heft—is a way
to weave together all three of those motivations and build coalitions that change society.

Mark Meckler was running a small law practice in Nevada
City, California, in early 2009 when he heard Rick Santelli's CNBC
on-air rant against Wall Street bailouts and the sweeping federal
responses to the housing and financial crisis. Santelli called for a
citizen uprising akin to the Tea Party. Meckler and his family answered the call, organizing an impromptu protest in Sacramento
that spring. A few weeks later, he co-founded an organization
called the Tea Party Patriots. It was a frenzied, purposeful time

of grassroots organizing. Before long, Meckler had become one of the main voices of the Tea Party movement nationwide.

The Tea Party itself has been effective at symbolizing its conservative cause, not least with the iconic "Don't Tread on Me" flag from the American Revolution. But almost from the start, the loose agglomeration of citizen-activist networks that carried the Tea Party label had an ambivalent, conflicted relationship with the Republican Party and its funders. As GOP leaders and their money and ideas machinery began to influence and even co-opt the movement, Meckler grew increasingly uncomfortable. Independent in party registration and temperament, he decided he had to leave the Tea Party Patriots.

So in 2012 he launched a new organization called Citizens for Self-Governance. And he defined CSG around two big fights. One was against the IRS, which he claimed had been biased against conservative and libertarian organizations. That fight has played out in the courts and in Congress. The second, playing out now in states across the country, was to call for a new constitutional convention.

This is not as quixotic as it sounds. Meckler's push for a convention of states under Article V of the Constitution is a very useful defining fight. It has a clear goal: to enact amendments that will rein in federal spending and regulation. It requires stepwise, coordinated action so that enough state legislatures pass resolutions in favor of a convention. Each fight in each legislature—and there *have* been fights—creates an organizing and fund-raising moment that makes abstract ideas about government overreach and corruption feel more real, and more solvable, to everyday citizens. CSG has even staged a simulated convention with legislators and scholars from around the country debating proposed amendments, to make the work feel more vividly urgent.

And most of all, the fight recapitulates the narrative of American revolution against concentrated power. With his proposed Article V convention of states, Meckler has found a way to convert hoary clichés about the Founders and Framers into a detailed action plan—one that the Founders and Framers actually provided us.

So, by the way, have the progressives who are calling for a constitutional amendment to undo the Supreme Court's *Citizens United* ruling on the constitutional role of money in politics. Like Meckler's convention of states, a campaign finance–reform amendment might not solve all the ills it purports to—and it may not ever come to pass. But the call to amend is potent because it symbolizes a range of issues and complaints about our corrupt system of elections and governance. It makes the invisible dimensions of that corruption visible.

The environmental activist and author Bill McKibben has a great instinct for making the invisible visible. McKibben is passionate about undoing man-made climate change. He knows the science thoroughly and can communicate it effectively. He knows, though, that climate change is such an all-encompassing, seemingly intractable issue that it can *disempower* many citizens. So he has chosen not to "boil the ocean," as the sadly apt saying goes, but rather to concentrate on a series of specific and emblematic battles.

McKibben was one of the most prominent leaders of the lobbying and direct action against construction of the Keystone XL pipeline. In that years-long and ultimately successful fight, he never pretended that stopping one pipeline was the solution to a systemic challenge. But killing Keystone gave committed activists and interested bystanders alike a concrete conflict in a defined arena with a binary possible outcome.

A more systemic fight he has picked is divestment. Through his organization 350.org (named for the threshold of parts per million of carbon in the atmosphere that marks planetary danger—a threshold we have already passed), McKibben has been organizing students on campuses around the country to push their college endowments to divest from companies in the fossil-fuel economy.

Using the model of divestment campaigns in the 1980s that helped pressure the South African regime to end apartheid, the "Fossil Free" divestment campaign practices some of the strategies we've examined. It describes a clear destination. It is based on a candid inventory of what the movement has (youthful energy, campuses, moral fervor) and what it lacks (the support of political or financial elites, camera-ready human conflicts, well-known villains). It proceeds from a shrewd understanding of the system of capital markets and university endowments and pension funds, and how that system is rigged for a way of measuring returns that externalizes the true costs of climate change.

But most important, it creates a fable in which many righteous smalls take on a few compromised bigs. It gives young citizens a purposeful way to challenge a visible authority. McKibben's critics often point out that divestment merely makes someone else an owner of the shares of fossil-fuel corporations. It is feel-good symbolism, they say. McKibben counters that divestment creates economic pressure on those companies and new social norms that will limit their room for maneuver. But he would also gladly grant that for the students, divestment *is* feel-good symbolism: *because it's important to feel good about one's cause, and because symbols matter.*

From this energy and emotion, McKibben has catalyzed bus tours, road shows, an all-star lecture and performance series, and a swirling ecosystem of joyful, creative campus-centered advocacy and protest campaigns. Philanthropies such as the Rockefeller Brothers Fund have agreed to divest, as have numerous pension funds and municipalities. According to 350.org, over 500 organizations with over $3 trillion in assets have also made divestment commitments. The moral of this fable is that fables can come to life.

PERSONIFY

McKibben is a well-known public figure. So well-known, in fact, that some of his adversaries from the fossil-fuel industry have decided to make *him* the issue. They have deployed stalkers to film McKibben in public, so they might catch him in a moment of "hypocrisy" like using a plastic bag. They have dug into his archived papers, looking to take quotes out of context and portray him as an unhinged extremist. They put these clips and excerpts online to damage his reputation.

This disturbing form of harassment frustrates McKibben, but he's acknowledged that it flatters him, too. It testifies to his effectiveness as a citizen. It is also an echo, albeit distorted and menacing, of his own advocacy efforts to personify climate denialism in the corporate person of ExxonMobil and the executives who run it.

Personifying a conflict means putting something abstract into human form. It is more than an ad hominem attack or the glorification of one individual. It is more even than making someone the "poster child" for an issue. It is finding a person or group of people whose own experience represents and stands in for the experience of all—and whose choices clarify for all the larger choices and stakes of the fight. It is a key part of challenging the self-justifying stories of the powerful.

In every state in the nation, the poor do not get equal access to justice. This is made painfully vivid when we consider the vast caseloads and overwhelmed staff of most legal aid programs and public defenders. Missouri ranks near the bottom in funding public defenders, and according to a 2014 study, its office of 376 such lawyers needs 270 more just to meet professional standards.

So when Governor Jay Nixon, a Democrat and former attorney general, again cut the level of approved funding, the state's chief public defender, Michael Barrett, could have done as plenty of beleaguered lawyers for the poor had done before him: sighed, swallowed his anger, and resigned himself to an even more brutal form of triage.

Instead, Barrett told a story in a symbolic act. He discovered a little-noticed emergency power in the state constitution, enabling him to draft any member of the state bar into service as a public defender. And he exercised the power on the governor, assigning him to represent a defendant accused of assault. In a letter to the governor, Barrett wrote, "It strikes me that I should begin with the one attorney in the state who not only created this problem, but is in a unique position to address it."

Nixon refused to heed this unusual summons—his office argued that Barrett acted outside his authority—but it didn't matter. Barrett's action became national news, and the governor had come to personify all that was broken with the state's criminal justice system. You could dismiss it as a stunt that changed nothing.

Or you could see it as a way to change the story and apply a new
source of pressure on the status quo. An emblematic fight matters
for reasons separate from its outcome.

That's what a remarkable group of twenty-one young environmental activists have discovered. With the help of the nonprofit Our Children's Trust, the youth have filed a lawsuit against
the Obama administration for, in essence, not saving the planet.
Their claim is that the federal government, by continuing to sub-
sidize fossil-fuel production, is failing in its "public trust" duty to
protect the atmosphere. The administration sought to get the suit
dismissed, arguing that it was taking active steps to address global
warming. But a federal magistrate allowed the suit to proceed.
Nervous oil companies then moved to intervene, contending that
the suit would force an "unprecedented restructuring of the economy" and "massive societal changes."

Which is exactly the goal of the young plaintiffs, who at the
time they filed suit ranged from eight to nineteen years old and
came from around the country. Among them are sixteen-year-old
Xiuhtezcatl Tonatiuh Martinez and seventeen-year-old Victoria
Barrett, Native American and African American, from Colorado
and New York. Both poised teens have become the face of the lawsuit, and they both embody the socially conscious spirit of their
multicultural cohort. They're comfortable folding the story of
their personal passion for environmental justice into the story of
their lawsuit into the story of their generation's responsibility.

Although the "atmospheric trust" doctrine their case relies
on is highly technical and, in the view of some legal experts, unlikely to prevail, the reality is that "twenty-one kids versus the
president of the United States" is a story line that the media has

found compelling—and it's an effective tool for garnering more support.

The same was true of the "Frisco Five." After a spate of police killings of unarmed people of color in San Francisco, several local activists in the spring of 2016 began a hunger strike at City Hall to call for the removal of the police chief. They were a telegenic group aged twenty-nine to sixty-six and they drew crowds of other protesters to City Hall each week, gaining a large following online.

With each day of protest and public attention, pressure increased on the mayor and city supervisors to back off their initial support for the chief. The hunger strike lasted seventeen tumultuous days, until the Frisco Five were so weak they had to be hospitalized. Immediately after the strike ended, hundreds of others organized more protests at City Hall. Five days later—and in the wake of yet another killing by a police officer—the chief resigned. Five not particularly well-known people, armed with nothing but a personified narrative of citizen power, had upended city politics.

Sometimes, it doesn't take even five people. It takes one. We saw that to bracing effect when Khizr Khan, the Muslim American lawyer and father of a U.S. Army captain killed in Iraq, denounced Donald Trump at the 2016 Democratic National Convention. More than any of Trump's electoral rivals, Khan was able to cut through the candidate's aura of outrageous impunity. By standing before tens of millions of Americans and excoriating Trump in accented English, pocket Constitution in hand, Khan put himself at some risk. And by putting himself at risk, he embodied the very story of sacrifice and true patriotism that he was telling. He occupied his own fable.

CRYSTALLIZE

Making your fight a fable makes the invisible dimensions of a situation visible. It can generate power to sustain long-term, even generational struggles—especially if you choose a fight that crystallizes your core principles. The gun-rights movement understands this. Some of its leaders have been as canny as McKibben and 350.org about activating students and using campuses to force defining conflicts and choices.

As the journalist Adam Weinstein has detailed, a small group of dedicated activists has been pushing "campus carry" policy proposals—allowing college students to carry concealed weapons—ever since the 2007 mass shooting on the Virginia Tech campus. But this group is not the NRA. In fact, it is increasingly at odds with the NRA. And its radical proposals—pushed in legislatures around the country—routinely fail, even in gun-friendly states. In Texas, for instance, where the governor signed a bill that allowed limited concealed-carry on public university campuses, this activist group has decried and disavowed the result as a weak compromise.

What is this group? Its public-facing form is called Students for Concealed Carry and claims more than 43,000 members in over 350 chapters across the United States. Behind SCC is an organization based outside Washington called the Leadership Institute (LI), which teaches basic tactics of political advocacy and organizing to young conservative and libertarian activists. And in partnership with LI is Gun Owners of America (GOA), a self-described "gundamentalist" organization that considers the NRA tame and Beltway-corrupted.

Weinstein, in a lengthy dispatch for the online magazine *The Trace*, describes how LI and GOA leaders have actively shaped SCC not only to become a tightly disciplined tactical operation but also to be the vanguard of a more ambitious and nearly evangelical strategy to purge the gun-rights cause of RINOs (Republicans in name only) who lack the stomach for ideological purity.

This is why SCC leaders seem unfazed by legislative setbacks, unbothered that on many of their campus-focused issues they are outnumbered by their critics. Campus carry is to them a means, not an end. It crystallizes and advances a broader agenda of no compromises. It is a fight that helps define a movement—or, in this case, make it more extreme. And if in the near term that fight brings only a string of defeats, its orchestrators are sanguine. To them, the consistency that generates a string of defeats will over the long term bring more true believers.

To juxtapose groups like 350.org and Students for Concealed Carry is not to suggest that they are equivalent in method, style, or social benefit. It is just to point out that you can effectively deploy power by picking useful and emblematic fights—and that these fights are often contests over what is "normal" in civic life.

Are such fights also, by definition, races to the extremes? Sometimes, if, as in the case of SCC, the strategic objective is ideological purification. But not always. Just as often, a defining fight can be a drive to claim the center. When advocates for undocumented immigrants had to choose a way to personify their push for comprehensive immigration reform, they chose the Dreamers: young people morally blameless for being brought here as children and morally praiseworthy for wanting to earn a college education or enter the armed services. Before gay activists litigated the issue of marriage, they too fought mightily for the chance to serve in the U.S. military.

There's nothing inherently right or wrong about pivoting to the right or left flank or to the center. That's a tactical choice. In all cases, though, choosing a battle that crystallizes the broader conflict—and defines it on your terms—is good strategy.

What's become known as the King County jail fight is a good illustration of this. In Seattle's Central District, which before gentrification was the city's core African American community, the county has long operated a juvenile youth detention center. When the King County government announced plans to tear it down and replace it with a state-of-the-art $210-million facility, a group consisting mainly of young people of color responded. Tear down the old one, yes, they said. *But do not replace it.*

The activists, members of a group called Ending the Prison-Industrial Complex (EPIC), argued that the youth jail was part of a broader system operating on autopilot to criminalize and incarcerate young people of color. They proposed to divert that $210 million away from the "school-to-prison pipeline" and into youth development, mentoring, jobs, crime prevention, and counseling. The county has said that the old jail is dilapidated and that it is simply unrealistic not to build a new one.

For years, the young people of EPIC have fought the government assiduously. They have organized multiracial, multigenerational marches and protests. They have shown up at City and County Council meetings to make impassioned pleas. They pushed the City Council to pass a resolution in support of their cause and forced the County Council to reduce the planned number of detention beds. They have persuaded philanthropies in town to help them develop blueprints for alternatives to more jails. They have filed suit to invalidate the county ballot measure that authorized the new building in the first place. They have been relentless.

The activists surely want to block the new jail. But more broadly, they want to use this conflict to shine a light on the systemic issues of youth incarceration in a putatively progressive county where 8 percent of youth but 50 percent of *detained* youth are black. They are not naïve, and they know that crime won't somehow stop if the new jail is blocked. But by reclaiming the narrative, they have exposed the moral vacuity of the government's defense of the status quo, perhaps best illustrated in the Orwellian name for the proposed facility: "The Children and Family Justice Center." Contrast that with the slogan often seen at EPIC actions: "No Children in Prison."

The outcome of this fight isn't yet known. But the outcome of the fight to *frame* the fight has already been settled. It's an EPIC victory. And a great case of crystallizing a complex struggle into a single, clear principle.

CHANGE THE EQUATION

STRATEGY 7: ACT EXPONENTIALLY

We come now to our final trio of strategies. *If people think power is finite and zero-sum, then you must change the equation.* You have to show them the possibility of positive-sum outcomes. The first strategy for doing that is to think and act in networks, so that your power is amplified not incrementally but exponentially. Networks enable us to create exponential power from thin air: by setting off contagions of attitude and action, by activating every citizen as a potential node of transmission, and by creating global webs of local knowledge and action.

CONTAGIONS OF GOOD ·

What makes this the age of networked power? Humans, after all, have always been enmeshed in networks. From the Silk Road to the slave trade, from the moment the disciples of Jesus began to spread the gospel, power has spread via networks.

What's different now, of course, is the speed and scale of the Internet. Today's networks are so visible and ubiquitous that they now shape how we see the world. From moguls to wannabe pop stars, everyone thinks in networks now. As Jeremy Heimans and Henry Timms have written, the emergence of the network not just as social infrastructure but also as mental model—a way to conceptualize life itself—means that we are imagining into being new forms of peer power that aren't top-down or zero-sum.

This kind of power doesn't scale up. It scales sideways, through open-source invitation rather than through control, coordination, or compulsion. Heimans and Timms call it "new power": the participatory "uploading" of power from a diffuse crowd, using modern social technologies. And Timms isn't just a theorist; he's a practitioner. He runs the 92nd Street Y in New York City, and in his tenure there has transformed an iconic Manhattan arts and civic institution into a global seedbed for civic innovation.

For instance, he is the mastermind behind #GivingTuesday, which makes the Tuesday after Thanksgiving a day to make gifts to nonprofits and social causes. The movement is a charity-centered response to Black Friday's materialism and the start of the holiday shopping season. When Timms and the 92Y team launched the first Giving Tuesday in October 2012, they had a hashtag, one month to prepare, and a few initial partners. They managed to generate over $10 million in gifts. Every year since, the amount has roughly doubled. By 2016, it was $168 million. And the number of participating donors and beneficiaries has grown on a similarly spectacular curve.

#GivingTuesday exploded into a global phenomenon not because Timms directed it but because he invited it. What made it contagious was not just the digital technology of Twitter and hashtags but also the social technology of an optimistic, counter-commercial value system. Those *values* were the virus that lit up the network.

Hashtags matter. So do the social media platforms that allow disaggregated people to combine their imagination and identities into a single political and cultural force. People who retweet surging memes, or who add their likes to the pile, are not necessarily "slacktivists" who are too lazy or inept to make "real" social change. They sometimes are part of a surge that can swell to great proportions and change the math of politics.

But talk of "going viral" is only the most superficial statement of what networks demand and permit, and of what a networked age truly is. It treats the network as an object, outside of us, something to nudge or to activate. The real goal for the practitioner of civic power isn't to nudge the network. It is to *be* the network.

Society becomes how you behave. That is a statement of network science: your behaviors and attitudes are contagious, rapidly and often imperceptibly. It is also a statement of ethics: your behaviors and attitudes are contagious, rapidly and often imperceptibly. The takeaway, either way, is that small actions (and omissions) compound. When you choose compassion or contempt, courtesy or discourtesy, civility or incivility, you begin a cascade of mimicry.

That's not to say everyone at all times has equal capacity to set off such contagions. It is to say if you are attuned to the ebb and flow of norms and energy in a social environment—as exquisitely attuned as a skillful artist or teacher—you will increase your odds of being catalytic when the moment is right. You will increase your odds of *making* the moment right.

When F. Willis Johnson became senior pastor of Wellspring Methodist Church on the corner of South Florissant and Wesley, half a block from police headquarters in Ferguson, Missouri, he did not plan on having to set a national example. It was chance and the force of events a few months later that brought a moment to his doorstep.

But because he was already sensitive to currents of credibility and identity in Ferguson, he knew what he had to do when Michael Brown was killed and the uprising began: throw open his church to angry protesters and make a space where they could be more than just angry. He waded into the protests to keep young black men from putting themselves in greater danger. He spoke bluntly to his flock and the press about Ferguson's problems. He has since launched a center for racial and economic justice that's attached to Wellspring. In all his work, he strives to make peace contagious.

Johnson does this the old-fashioned way. By ministering to people face-to-face. By "holding up his corner," as he puts it. He is not particularly active on social media, even though he is a relatively young pastor. And though he himself got a burst of national press when a photo of him calming an enraged protester did in fact go viral, he does not try to build an online following.

Instead, in his Center for Social Empowerment and through his sermons and his teaching, Johnson is activating an *analog* network. It's based on the principle of interrelatedness. He maps power and inequity in Ferguson and North St. Louis County and is helping his congregants identify in data what they have always felt in their bones.

He cultivates relationships with allies around the city and the state. He tutors a young generation of would-be local leaders who don't yet have the social capital or experience to become skillful advocates or citizens. And he brings in outsiders from every part of his life journey—which spans many states and many churches and many schools and many neighborhoods—who might have skills to share with the youth he serves.

There is no longer unrest or rioting in Ferguson. When you drive down Canfield Street, where Darren Wilson killed Michael Brown and where Brown's body lay in the street for hours, it is empty but for the remnants of a makeshift memorial. The town is strangely quiet. It has lapsed back into a sleepy and segregated stasis that reminds you peace is not merely the absence of war.

True peace requires a sense of purpose and place—a feeling that *I'm part of something greater and it is to be found right here.* Willis Johnson knows this. He models it, by holding up his corner. And by the power of his example and of his network, he is spreading it.

EVERY CITIZEN AN EPIDEMIOLOGIST

In the Marine Corps, there is a core principle that can be summarized thus: "Every Marine a rifleman." No matter what your occupational specialty—tank mechanic, cook, supply officer, scout—the U.S. Marine Corps expects you to be ready to fight, which means having good marksmanship and thinking like a front-line infantry rifleman.

Civic power operates on a similar principle—the ability to convert any citizen into an active member of the team at any time. But the skills required for civic power more nearly resemble those of an epidemiologist: the ability to read a map of the spread of a virus, or to locate the concentrated centers of its activity, or to focus energy on containing it. But of course, in civic power, the virus isn't always a disease—it might be an economic trend, or a spate of violence, or a growing social consensus on an issue. No matter what it is, if it's happening, we can sense it. All of us can try to think, see, and act like an epidemiologist.

Take Dr. Leana Wen, the public-health director for Baltimore, who has become a beacon of hope in her struggling city. In one notable initiative, her department has deployed ex-felons to be human antennae in the most violent neighborhoods, to build relationships block by block, anticipate the next outbreak of violence, and intervene. The ex-felons have standing to move freely, and they internalize and update the network map as they walk the beat.

And of course you don't have to be an actual epidemiologist to exercise this kind of citizen power. You just have to hold in mind a big-picture view of your ecosystem. From that vantage point, identify key nodes of transmission. Then act upon or act with those nodes. Act to influence them, to infect them, to replace them or to displace them.

And remember that networks do not eliminate inequality of power. In many cases they exacerbate it. Uber is a pure example.

Here's a business model made possible entirely by networked technologies that treat workers and customers as floating atoms waiting for a call that will instantly link them together. For the rider, Uber brings seamless convenience to urban transportation.

But the profits that are unleashed by this disaggregation of middlemen taxi companies are not shared or circulated evenly. Isolated individual drivers are contingent contractors at the mercy of the company. They have little recourse when the company pushes fares (and thus wages) downward. They are easily replaced. And Uber is able to deploy its various forms of scaled power, from its vast web of customers to its major investors to its superstar lobbyists, to bypass or dominate governments that try to regulate it.

So an epidemiologist's approach to rebalancing the power equation in the case of Uber must start with using networks against it. Only a fraction of Uber drivers has organized to push for better pay and working conditions. In New York City, a group of over 1,000 drivers has formed a "solidarity organization." It's short of a union (which, as non-employees, they are barred from creating) and is therefore unable to bargain wages collectively. But it can apply focused pressure, both inside and outside, on the company.

This networked organization, like other driver associations that Uber has had to accept in order to settle class-action lawsuits in California and elsewhere, will be able to map—and build—driver power. It can provide the backbone for other forms of worker-centered activity beyond expressing grievances—for instance, delivering portable, prorated health and retirement benefits to drivers.

This highlights something else the citizen-epidemiologist does: design networks in ways that maximize people power. Consider the design of TED and TEDx. Both are world-renowned brands because TED Talks are ubiquitous. But they have very different architectures. TED is centered around an expensive, exclusive annual event in Vancouver. TEDx is an open platform that enables people in any community in the world, following only a few basic rules, to create their own TED-like convenings.

Regulating access to a closed network—the way TED founder Chris Anderson does by running the mother-ship TED conference—generates a certain kind of power. It's the power of cachet and scarcity. But opening the network to an uncapped number of new nodes—the way Anderson did by creating the TEDx ecosystem—generates exponentially more power. And this is the power of inclusion and abundance.

There are civic TEDx opportunities all around us—opportunities to design networks guided by core operating principles that can otherwise be tailored by anyone anywhere to respond to local circumstances. And we can activate these networks not only for collective inspiration, the way TEDx does, but also for collective action.

NETWORKED LOCALISM

The anthropologist James Scott writes about *metis*, a Greek word that means *practical knowledge* and *local insight*. His classic book, *Seeing Like a State*, describes how the modern administrative state is designed to look at people from above and from a remove. The worst-case results are Stalinism and the catastrophic Five-Year Plans; more commonplace are stupid bureaucracies that treat citizens like nonhuman inputs.

Scott flips the model for decision-making and power, saying it should proceed from the *metis* of the nearby, not the *hubris* of the distant. In a complex system, local insight is the key to adaptability. Trust people closest to the problem to come up with the most useful ways to solve the problem—indeed, to see it.

Mauricio Lim Miller used to run the California state welfare agency until he came to believe he was making things worse for his clients *because* he saw them as clients. Not as citizens, or creators, or problem solvers. The system he ran was blind to the social capital and resourcefulness of poor people. "There's no such thing as a single mother," Lim Miller often says, meaning every single mother relies on a network of help to get by.

So he gave Governor Jerry Brown his letter of resignation and he set off to create the Family Independence Initiative. FII supports and organizes low-income families so that they can tap into their own capacity for economic and civic health. Its method is very simple, and very difficult. FII staff gives the families baseline funds—up to $200 for reporting small steps taken to reduce debt or get education or the like—and requires them to meet as a group at least monthly. Then the staff get out of the way.

Trusting the network to support each other—with ideas, time, emotional support, fixes, and the *metis* of local common sense— puts the families in the "power position," as Lim Miller has said. But then adamantly refusing to "help" them if they flounder: that's hard. It's the FII way. And it works. Among FII families, household income increases substantially. Use of government subsidies for housing and food fall substantially, as does debt. Participants start businesses, buy homes, and solidify their lives.

Lim Miller's innovation has earned him awards and accolades, including a MacArthur "genius" grant, but he reflexively steps out of the way to highlight the families. They're the ones who come up with solutions. They're the ones who practice power from the bottom up, bypassing or preempting the state, in ways that don't fit easily into a left-right framework. They are the ones creating a sense of agency where it did not exist before.

FII operates in six cities—Philadelphia, New Orleans, Phoenix, Oakland, San Francisco, and Boston. As it has grown and begun experimenting with matched savings accounts, lending circles, and other tools for social mobility, the staff and families relentlessly collect data on what works and circulate their findings with one another. This cross-city network for learning is the key to FII's success.

And it's the wave of the future. All citizenship is local. But *networked* localism, trying new things not in isolation but in collaboration, is a sign of our times. When the Bush administration decided in 2007 not to accede to the Kyoto Protocols, a global network of city leaders decided to commit to meeting the protocol's carbon reduction targets together. That template has since been replicated on the minimum wage and paid sick leave, bike lanes and housing affordability, gun violence and gay marriage. Lawmakers and activists are sharing policy experiments, successes, lessons learned.

All these citizens, united, are making a web, a great archipelago of power that can bypass brokenness and monopolies. Networked localism shifts the equation of power away from a dysfunctional national government. Many smalls can surpass a few bigs, and many locals can outdo a few faraways—if the small and the local are woven together into a well-made network. Whether at the level of the city or the citizen, that's how you generate power exponentially.

STRATEGY 8: ACT RECIPROCALLY

If people think power is finite and zero-sum, then you must change the equation. You have to show that getting involved is a win-win, not a sucker's game. The next strategy for doing that is to act reciprocally: to give your power to those who will give it back—with interest. Creating power this way means building systems of mutual aid and then opening up opportunities for deep, cooperative self-government.

BE LIKE BEN

Benjamin Franklin was a club-maker to the core. At age twenty-one he created the Junto, a discussion group for "like minded aspiring artisans and tradesmen who hoped to improve themselves while they improved their community." Junto-style circles would soon proliferate across Philadelphia. Later he created the country's first subscription library (which immediately spawned many more), Philadelphia's first volunteer fire department, the Pennsylvania militia, the American Philosophical Society, and the precursor to the University of Pennsylvania.

Franklin was by nature sociable and entrepreneurial, with a rare talent for generating something from nothing. He conducted all this club-making and civic innovation with a cheeky spirit of defiance toward the political and religious establishment. It was also good for his printing and publishing business. As Walter Isaacson recounts in his celebrated Franklin biography, the man was a living amalgam of the two great strands of American DNA: enterprising individualism and earnest communitarianism. Franklin's life proved that these were not in conflict; that, in fact, democratic citizenship required both.

So here is a simple precept for anyone who wants to change the equation of power in a community: Be like Ben.

That entails looking at an absence of opportunities for citizen participation not as a problem but as an opportunity—to invent, and fill the void. It entails inviting people with a playful spirit and setting in motion perpetual cycles of reciprocity. It entails mixing friendship and benefit in group activity that stirs the heart as much as the mind. It entails organizing, tirelessly, and making spaces where others can organize themselves.

The scholar David Singh Grewal, in his book *Network Power*, makes an interesting distinction between power as *sovereignty* and as *sociability*. Power-as-sovereignty is expressed through structures of government and corporate action designed for rule and direction. Power-as-sociability emerges from countless uncoordinated interactions and choices that are happening side by side, simultaneously. On funding platforms such as Kiva and Kickstarter and co-creation platforms such as Etsy or Wikipedia, people choose to join and then power flows collaboratively across the network in self-organizing ways.

Franklin in his career held positions of power-as-sovereignty. He was postmaster of Philadelphia, a member of the Pennsylvania Assembly, U.S. ambassador to France. But his was the power of sociability—his winning personality, yes, but also his genius for creating platforms for creation that others could co-own and expand.

My own work has been guided by Franklin's example. A few years ago, I looked at the national ecosystem of groups and leaders working on civic engagement and saw a hole. Everywhere there were organizations focused on issues or constituencies, whether veterans or immigrant rights or civic education or voting or racial inclusion, each in their own professional community, separated by invisible fences of habit and culture. I realized my nonprofit, Citizen University, didn't belong to any particular fiefdom. My team and I had relationships across all of them. We were uniquely placed to address this civic market failure and to do something *for the good of the realm.*

So in 2011 we formed the Civic Collaboratory, a national network of over 150 civic innovators drawn from across the political landscape and from all those various subdomains of citizenship-related work. The name "Collaboratory" was intended to convey the spirit of experimenting, together. I invited retired Supreme Court Justice Sandra Day O'Connor and Bill Gates Sr. to join me to convene the first meeting. Very few people turned down our invitation. We met that summer at the Seattle headquarters of the Gates Foundation.

And there we learned that simply starting something where nothing existed is not enough to change the equation. We spent a day discussing ways that people across all these silos could collaborate more effectively. With my friendly but firm prodding, we explored whether this remarkable group could all get behind a single goal or project.

My prodding was not enough, it turned out. By the end of the day, though the participants were excited to be in such catalytic company, an air of unreality had set in. Talk of getting behind a common project was nice, when in the confines of this retreat setting, but everyone was beginning to sense what would happen the next day: they would realize it would not really be in their direct interest to commit to such a common endeavor. No one would be funded for it, and it would just eat up time and resources.

So for the second meeting of the Collaboratory, my team and I flipped the proposition. Instead of asking people to come as altruists, we invited them to come in the spirit of mutual self-interest. We created a new convening format, borrowed from low-income immigrant entrepreneurs. Because they often lack access to traditional bank lending, they will circle up with a co-ethnic group of immigrants and pool their savings into a common pot. Then they'll take turns getting the whole pot to capitalize their minimart or restaurant or other small business.

Our format, adapted from this practice, is called the Rotating Credit Club. At every quarterly Collaboratory meeting, five or six members get to be "in rotation." They present to the rest of the group a project they are trying to launch or a challenge they are trying to solve. And the rest of the group offers more than commentary or critique. We make commitments of help. We make investments of capital in our colleagues—institutional, intellectual, relationship, sometimes even financial capital. My job as curator is to draw out these commitments. But it's not hard. In this new format, everyone is motivated to lean forward and offer help.

Why? Because *what goes around comes around.* It behooves you to make and keep commitments now because in one or two quarters you'll ask me to do the same for you. And I will. Designing a system around this dynamic changed everything. It opened up a channel of energy—of collective power and mutual aid—that had been closed when we first met. It moved us from zero-sum to positive-sum mindsets.

In the five years since that stalled first meeting, the Civic Collaboratory has become more than a networking group. It has become a mutual-aid society within which we nurture bonds of trust and affection. It has become an incubator of creative partnerships among strange bedfellows. We see ourselves as the backbone of a cross-partisan movement to revitalize citizenship in the United States.

And in true Ben Franklin spirit, we have spawned more such mutual-aid societies. Other groups, from veterans organizations to foundations to museums to Hollywood agencies, have asked Citizen University if they could borrow our approach. Our reply: "Take it. It's our gift." Our aim is not to hoard the method we've developed. It is to propagate it. And now with a wide range of partners, we are creating youth-centered and immigrant-centered collaboratories, as well as city-based ones, to bring new people into circles of power and to enable them to devise ventures no one could have planned or predicted.

DEEP COOPERATION

The spirit of reciprocal giving I have just described requires trust. But here's the thing: it also *creates* trust. And if there is a chicken-and-egg quandary over where to begin, the experience of Franklin and every other civic catalyst in American history says simply to begin by trusting. You create trust by trusting. You earn trust by giving it.

Franklin's example also teaches us that it's important to open up opportunities for citizens to practice cooperative self-government. Not at the surface level of voting or signing petitions or even protesting. But in deeper ways where we are responsible for making things work and where, if something goes wrong, there is no one else to blame but the defined circle of *us* that we affirmatively joined.

One exciting case study of deep self-government is participatory budgeting (PB). This is a movement that began in Porto Alegre, Brazil, over thirty years ago and has now spread to cities around the world. In PB, local governments set aside a chunk of the municipal budget that will be allocated by a panel of citizens rather than by elected officials or their staff. Those citizens then get to—or, rather, have to—generate project ideas, deliberate on them, negotiate priorities, and commit their finite funds against those priorities.

The method has now spread to over 3,000 cities worldwide, including fifteen in the United States since 2009. "Real money, real power" is the movement's slogan. In some cities, like Greensboro, North Carolina, PB has been opened up to residents citywide, giving them both a stake in the action and a place to practice power. In others, like Seattle, PB has been applied specifically as a form of *youth* civic empowerment.

Thus far the experiments have engaged over 150,000 people in deciding how to spend over $145 million. In the grand scheme of public budgets ("a billion here, a billion there, and pretty soon you're talking about real money"), these are still not large numbers.

But the better measure of the way PB has altered the equation of power is to think in terms of the conduits of any city's power structure. The *institution* of budgeting, once the preserve of a priesthood of experts, has been opened up. Unwritten *codes* about how policy making and public process are supposed to unfold have been altered. *Organizations* that bring together voiceless outsiders have gained a seat at the budget-making table. They've created a global *network* of practice and learning, and as they've done so they have spread new *narratives* about how citizens relate to their city.

By subtly reorienting power structures, the PB movement has set itself up for more growth and scale. No one who tries participatory budgeting ever wants less of it. PB is a remedy for citizen apathy and alienation. It's a new form of social identity that's based on participation and deciding. You see that especially among young people who are proud to be *deciders*.

A pioneering Chicago-based organization called the Mikva Challenge has also demonstrated the power of inviting young people into power. It's named after Abner Mikva, the former congressman, federal judge, and White House counsel who "retired" roughly the way Ben Franklin did: by creating new civic platforms for participation. The Mikva Challenge teaches what it calls "action civics"—learning power by practicing it.

High school students in Mikva programs lobby aldermen for policy change or funding. They serve on city commissions to press the school district or the mayor's office for better programs. They run peacemaking projects with the police and community groups. And they do all this through the schools, as part of the curriculum. They learn citizenship through direct experience and structured reflection. When their teachers or the adults in government trust them to come up with useful ideas, they prove worthy of the trust, which sets in motion a positive feedback loop of real-life skill-building.

Of course, deep self-government isn't only about interacting with public bureaucracies. It is about cultivating habits of cooperation in every circle of our lives.

Bob Woodson, the blunt-speaking seventy-seven-year-old founder of the Center for Neighborhood Enterprise, has spent decades organizing poor people, particularly African Americans, in communities wracked by poverty, disorder, and violence. CNE's operating philosophy is to transform people and places "from the inside out." Self-government, in Woodson's world, begins with the self: gaining command of one's own life choices, often with the support of faith organizations, and creating ripples of responsibility that spread outward.

The work of CNE is similar in spirit and method to that of FII. And like Mauricio Lim Miller, Woodson has won a MacArthur genius award for his work. Unlike him, he has become a mentor on issues of urban poverty to conservative politicians such as Paul Ryan. But Woodson is no partisan. He's worked at both the progressive Urban League and the conservative American Enterprise Institute. He participated in President Obama's My Brother's Keeper initiative to support men and boys of color. And he is blunt about the fact that during the Jim Crow years of his youth and the civil rights movement, "limited government" was not the friend of a black man like him; the federal government was.

Now, however, he sees many federal programs as an obstacle to the kind of bottom-up renewal he and his team are seeding in Milwaukee, Newark, Washington, Indianapolis, and other cities around the country. CNE activates churches, kinship networks, and local businesses to invite the residents of these hard-hit cities to help each other: to place children whom the foster-care system doesn't; to help ex-offenders become contributing neighbors; to build the relationships that can head off violent crime.

Collective action and cooperation are words more often associated with the left than the right. Woodson is utterly pragmatic about it. Cooperation works. Mutuality works. Acting reciprocally is empowering not only because it obligates other people into a social contract but also because it reminds us that our own power is a gift. When as citizens we choose to give our power to people and institutions that will hoard or abuse or misplace it, we contribute to the problem. If we choose to exchange our power with people and institutions that will cycle it back to us, we contribute to the solution.

Consider the emergence of health-care sharing ministries, in which hundreds of thousands of evangelical Christians around the United States have opted out of the traditional health-insurance system (and, pointedly, the mandates of the Affordable Care Act) in order to create their own mutual-aid medical networks. The members pay dues and cover each other's costs. They make decisions together about what they can and cannot cover, and how to manage their collective funds. The sharing ministries have grown by word of mouth, with membership more than doubling in the last seven years.

In parallel, consider the growth of the cooperative economy in the United States. Cooperatives are businesses owned by the workers or customers or producers, and they are run democratically. There are now about 30,000 in the United States, an increase of nearly 50 percent since 2005. And the ecosystem is becoming more diverse and sophisticated. In the Bay Area, groups such as the Sustainable Economies Law Center are now creating legal infrastructure to support local cooperatives for shared food production, housing, finance, and renewable energy.

Health-care sharing ministries and cooperatives have in common a commitment to changing the locus of responsibility. For members of both, there is no such thing as "someone else's problem." You might, depending on your worldview, consider one or the other unrealistic or even dangerous. Sharing ministries won't cover certain procedures, including abortion and some reproductive health care. They sometimes can't cover the costs of extraordinary health problems. Cooperatives, meanwhile, can be cumbersome to manage and difficult to scale. The cooperative economy doesn't value efficiency as much as traditional corporate capitalism does.

But platforms like these generate peer power by giving their members the mutual responsibility of making things work. Which gives their members the practice and experience of making *sure* things work. Which gives them more control over their own lives and outcomes. The cliché is that "with great power comes great responsibility." We should remember that the converse is also true: with great responsibility can come great power.

STRATEGY 9: PERFORM POWER

If people think power is finite and zero-sum, then you must change the equation. Remind yourself and others that power is in fact infinite—that we can create it where it does not exist. Our final strategy for doing that is simply this: act powerful. When we act powerful we become powerful. That plays out in the poses and stances we strike in civic life, in the art we make together in everyday life, and in the reality of minority rule.

THE POSE OF POWER

In one of the most popular TED Talks ever, the Harvard social psychologist Amy Cuddy shows that "power poses"—stances and facial expressions that communicate personal power and confidence—are self-fulfilling. She shows it by describing her deep experimental research into the social effects of stance and physical presence. But mainly she shows it by showing it: by striking poses like Wonder Woman (hands on hips, legs shoulder-width apart, steady gaze) and inviting the audience to do the same.

The effect is not just exhilarating, it's infectious. As people look around at each other while holding the pose and feeling bigger than they did a moment earlier, they are almost giddy with the sensation of having made power out of thin air.

It would be simplistic to summarize Cuddy's fascinating work, or the comparable work of the pioneering Berkeley social psychologist Dacher Keltner, as "fake it till you make it." But there is certainly a core of truth to the maxim. The appearance of belief in oneself begets the reality of it. Acting as if you were worthy of respect can make you so.

Not surprisingly, professional women have especially been drawn to Cuddy's message. Sheryl Sandberg has made the message part of her "Lean In" campaign. But the popularity of power poses as a form of workplace self-help also highlights the risk of focusing attention on the individual. Although it's true that a young woman in a corporate workplace can help herself by avoiding a posture of self-doubt and self-effacement, it's also true that in many corporate settings there are *structural* forces of bias and closed networks that keep women from keeping pace with men in earnings and promotions.

That doesn't cancel out the importance of power poses. It means simply that we have to apply the principle at a larger scale. Just as there is individual body language, there is something we might call "body-politic language"—the way the posture of a *group* can communicate collective belief and generate collective power.

This is how Occupy Wall Street went from a rhetorical headline in the Canadian newspaper *Adbusters* to a physical occupation of Zuccotti Park in lower Manhattan—then spread to other city plazas and "power spaces" around the country. It's why Senator Chris Murphy's 2016 filibuster to secure a vote on gun reform legislation led, days later, to a dramatic sit-in by Democratic members of Congress on the floor of the House. GOP leaders unintentionally made it a bigger phenomenon when they shut off House cameras, leading members to broadcast what now felt like *censored* theater via Periscope. True, neither the filibuster nor the sit-in achieved passage of the desired bills. But they communicated a stance of defiance against the status quo, which gave new energy to activists and new urgency to addressing gun violence.

To "fake it till you make it" as a *we* and not just a *me* requires a spirit of theatricality: attention-grabbing, suspenseful *collective* performance.

Annie Leonard, the director of Greenpeace USA, has long been fighting oil companies that want to drill in the Arctic. When Shell in 2015 sent a massive drilling rig to the port of Seattle to get fitted for Arctic drilling, some activists focused on the inside game of pushing port and city officials to delay or deny permits to the company. Leonard's team and many partners came up with an exhilarating outside game, catalyzing one of the most vivid spectacles of recent citizen activism.

Over the course of several days, hundreds of protesters paddled colorful kayaks, canoes, rafts, and other watercraft, including a large Duwamish canoe, to surround the rig and prevent it from docking. They were dubbed the "kayaktivists," and images of the makeshift rainbow flotilla spread around the world. Four months later, Shell announced that it was abandoning Arctic drilling altogether. The activists who amassed in 2016 to block the Dakota Access pipeline—especially the Standing Rock Sioux, who memorably charged on horseback to protect their sacred land and water—used the same playbook. The theatricality of the Standing Rock encampment and protests activated Native Americans from tribes across the continent and allies from around the world.

When we look at this era's campus activism, the most effective action has tapped into this same awareness of stance and theatricality. At Yale, this has been true on both the left and right.

Progressive students in 2015 orchestrated powerful visual spectacles to pressure the administration to address racial inequity and insensitivity on campus. In Calhoun College, for instance, the Yale residence hall named after the white supremacist and disunionist South Carolina senator John C. Calhoun (class of 1804), students planted a field of tombstone-like protest signs, each bearing the Calhoun College seal and the name of a student who wanted the college's name changed.

But the controversies at Yale have also included debates about free expression and whether some advocates for racial inclusion were practicing their own brand of intolerance. The students of the Buckley Program, named after the proto-conservative writer William F. Buckley Jr. (class of 1950), responded in a creative way. They organized the first-ever "Disinvitation Dinner," an event to honor speakers who had been disinvited by progressive colleges because they'd expressed controversial opinions. George Will was the inaugural honoree. Ayaan Hirsi Ali and former NYPD Commissioner Ray Kelly have since followed. The black-tie dinner, held in Manhattan, has the air of a performance. Because it *is* one. It's meant to be noticed.

Beyond campus life, think of some of the inflection points in the debates about Confederate symbols in the South or police brutality in our cities. Picture Bree Newsome, the thirty-year-old African American artist who, like a superhero, scaled the flagpole at the state capitol in Columbia, South Carolina, to remove the Confederate flag. As she took it down, she intoned: "You come against me with hatred and oppression and violence. I come against you in the name of God. This flag comes down today!" When she was arrested, she smiled broadly and recited the Lord's Prayer.

Or picture Ieshia Evans, a thirty-five-year-old African American nurse and mother who participated in the Baton Rouge protests after the police killing of Alton Sterling. Wearing a flowing sundress with her hands folded before her, she walked calmly to face two rifle-wielding cops in riot gear. In a now-iconic photo of the moment, the helmeted officers, faces obscured, rush toward her and seem off-balance; behind them on the left side of the image is a phalanx of armored officers. To the right, Evans stands placidly alone, her dress trailing behind as if she had walked in from a fairy tale.

Are these stunts? Of course they are. They generate power by stirring the imagination and affinity of many unseen others. In each case a courageous, self-possessed individual is the focus of our attention, but in each case that individual has emerged from a community in action. Neither woman seems alone. Nor do we when we watch them.

But sometimes committing to a power pose is not a matter of theatricality. It is a matter of necessity. Patty Stonefish, a martial arts teacher in Fargo, North Dakota, combines her knowledge of taekwondo with elements of her Lakota heritage to lead unique self-defense workshops for Native American women. About one-third of Native women are raped in their lifetime; worse, these rapes are rarely prosecuted. So on one level, as *YES! Magazine* has reported, Stonefish's workshops teach basic martial arts skills that any woman can use to face an attacker.

On another level, the workshops are about rediscovering power. Every principle of physical self-defense, Stonefish says, can be applied to a broader agenda of emotional and civic re-empowerment. It is life-changing for her students to discover that with the proper stance and mindset, they can upend a much larger foe. It's a realization that helps them help themselves—and others—in their relationships, workplaces, and communities. As Stonefish has said, "I wanted women to rediscover what's powerful in themselves." To show their strength—and thus make more.

MAKE ART, THEN POWER

It is no accident that theater and democracy came into being at the same time in Athens. Both involve yanking the individual out of the enclosure of the private self. Both involve rituals of shared public experience. Both involve bringing the imagination to life in a way that reminds us that *all* our bonds are imagined.

Gregg Mozgala is a young theater artist in New York City who looks like plenty of other young theater artists: a little scruffy, with soulful eyes. But in person he is not like most others. He has cerebral palsy and walks with a pronounced limp (his wry professional tagline is "Actor. Writer. Cripple"). And as he pursued his creative calling, he found that there were no theater companies that created works by or for artists with disabilities. So he created one. The Apothetae, a theater company named after the chasm in ancient Greece where deformed and disabled babies were left to die, commissions new plays by artists with disabilities and stages them with ability-integrated casts.

Gregg's aim with The Apothetae is not just to provide more opportunity for disabled artists. It is, more fundamentally, to bring to theater audiences fully realized and complex visions of the "disabled experience" and to set in motion a shift in social norms and laws. It is to convert identity—the label of disability—into community, and to expand that community to include allies moved empathically by art.

We know, of course, from television and movies that popular culture can shape such shifts in attitudes. Many activists have noted that gay marriage became a reality in part because a generation ago the NBC sitcom *Will and Grace* introduced millions of Americans to relatable gay characters. (On the negative side of the ledger, Fox's show *COPS* reinforced images of black criminality for twenty-five years until the advocacy group ColorOfChange.org pressured the network to take it off the air.) And other shows on the air today, like ABC's *Black-ish* and *Fresh Off the Boat*, are obliterating stereotypes about African American and Asian American families.

But few of us have the platform to create broadcast television shows. Fortunately, anyone anywhere can use art to create power. A Twin Cities nonprofit called Springboard for the Arts runs a program called Creative Exchange that asks artists around the country to create playful "toolkits" in response to citizen requests. How can I generate foot traffic to local businesses during a street construction project? How can I get neighborhoods across the city to collaborate? How can I get to know the people on my street? The "answers" have ranged from pop-up galleries to five-hundred-person communal meals to sculptural bike racks—and the tools to replicate those projects anywhere.

These citizen-artist collaborations all proceed from the idea that if you *perform* power, you create it. In the same spirit, my organization, Citizen University, worked with artists, designers, activists, and neighbors in Akron, Miami, Philadelphia, and Wichita on a project called "The Joy of Voting."

Its purpose is to create (or re-create) what used to exist in urban political life before the advent of television: a robust, festal, participatory culture around voting and elections. Street theater, open-air debates, dueling parades and bands. In Miami that means all-night parties with hot DJs, where the only way to get in is to show you're registered. In Akron it means performing political plays in the bed of a pickup truck that goes from neighborhood to neighborhood. In Philly it's a voting-themed scavenger hunt through colonial Old Town. In Wichita, it's creating mixtapes in the North End and live graffiti-art to get out the vote.

Our philosophy is that voting shouldn't be *Eat your vegetables*; it should be *Join the club*. Or, better yet, *Join the party*. And the same is true of citizenship in general. There is an art to making a bigger club. It often involves making art.

The writer Terry Tempest Williams tells in her gorgeous memoir, *When Women Were Birds,* of trying in the 1990s to get members of her conservative Utah congressional delegation behind a "Citizens' Proposal" to protect millions of acres of wilderness. She is rebuffed, then told at a subcommittee hearing, "There is something about your voice I cannot hear." Although the congressman who said this to her was referring to the sound quality of her microphone, his words became a metaphor.

Discouraged, Williams decided she had to turn to her art—and to other creators. So she and a few allies compiled a collection of essays by well-known writers about the West and published 1,000 copies. They called it *Testimony*. She went back to Washington and gave the anthology to members of Congress and the media as a way to make her case. A reporter told her she was being colossally naïve. Indeed, Congress did nothing. But a copy had gotten in the hands of Hillary Clinton, who gave it to her husband. A year later, President Bill Clinton took executive action, creating the new Grand Staircase–Escalante National Monument and protecting over 2 million acres of Utah wilderness. "This little book," he told her later, "made a difference."

MINORITY RULE

Any performance of power begins in the imagination. It begins with your capacity to visualize no longer being beaten down or ignored or unheard. From there it blossoms into your capacity to act *as if* you already had the social and civic power you seek—and *as if* you had attained that power on your terms, not by bending to majority norms.

Remember: A democracy governs by majority rule, but it is moved by minority will. In every instance of significant civic change, it is the *majority* that bends to a *minority*.

When we talk of the "will of the people" or ask whether there is "popular will" for change, we are never talking about all the people or even most of them. We are always talking about a minority—an activated, effective minority of people who act bigger than they are, change the agenda and narrative, and eventually move attitudes and beliefs enough to get a numerical majority of citizens to agree with or at least tolerate their stance.

According to voter turnout data from the 2016 presidential primaries, just 9 percent of all Americans made Hillary Clinton and Donald Trump the major-party nominees. In most local elections in the United States, the turnout of eligible voters ranges from single digits to 20 percent. They are the ones who decide. Their preferences advance. The minority that shows up, goes up.

Consider that when Tea Party activists began in 2010 to mobilize by conference call and social media, they were never a majority even among Republicans. They weren't even a majority of the people who attended congressional town meetings. They were simply the organized. You don't need a majority to wield power. You need a demand, and you need to put it in motion in ways that others can join.

Consider that in Verden, Germany, a sole activist shod in Birkenstocks has created a worldwide coalition of citizens to push against the Transatlantic Trade and Investment Partnership. Felix Kolb does not have the institutional might of the unions or think tanks that have blocked a similar multinational trade deal in the United States. But he co-founded a mighty grassroots organization called Campact—combining "campaign" and "action"—that has now mobilized hundreds of thousands of Germans to pressure national decision-makers and put the deal's backers on defense.

Consider the Montgomery, Alabama, bus boycott of 1955–1956. Black citizens organized to withhold their dollars from a public transportation system that seated and treated them as second-class. Their boycott helped change social attitudes and ultimately the law. It remade the narrative and cleared the way for other challenges to Jim Crow elsewhere. But at no time were boycotters a majority in the city, just as at no time in the civil rights movement did a majority of the country approve of its tactics. It only takes a few.

More to the point, it *always* takes only a few.

This is one of the most easily forgotten facts of American civic life. It is one of the most central reasons that you are more powerful than you think. And it is why the strategy of performing power means believing in the outsize power of the outnumbered.

A century ago the temperance movement, led by a motivated "moral minority," transformed the United States. In his engrossing history *Last Call*, Daniel Okrent details how the Women's Christian Temperance Union and then the Anti-Saloon League took command of the country's power structure to make Prohibition a reality. At a time when the average American adult drank seven gallons of pure alcohol a year (three times more than today), those activists did not cater to mainstream norms. They decried them.

The Anti-Saloon League's leader, Wayne Wheeler, felt the reformist fervor of his religious, heavily female activist ranks. But he had a unique and wizardly capacity to organize and communicate—and with cold-blooded instincts he put together a political army more potent in his time than the NRA has been in ours.

"[A]s practiced by the ASL," writes Okrent, "democracy was a form of coercion. . . . The ASL did not seek to win majorities; it played on the margins, aware that if it could control, say, one-tenth of the voters in any close race, it could determine the outcome." By mobilizing a web of Protestant churches, and firing them up with apocalyptic rhetoric about the evils of alcohol, the ASL could activate tens of thousands of citizens to show up at rallies, oust "wet" governors and legislators, push for "dry" ordinances, pass the collection plate, and generally whip up an anti-alcohol frenzy that became widespread.

184 | YOU'RE MORE POWERFUL THAN YOU THINK

The rest, as they say, is history—the ratification of the Eighteenth Amendment, which banned alcoholic beverages in the United States; the underground resistance to Prohibition; then finally its repeal fourteen years later. But the history that's relevant here is that the ASL began as a small force that acted big—and then became big.

So the question today is what group of citizens is similarly small? What insistent minority can imagine itself as the majority? And make it so?

Maybe it'll be open-carry activists. Maybe it'll be transgender-rights activists. Maybe it'll be Socialists. Maybe it'll be libertarians. Maybe it'll be people who want your town to be friendlier to developers and big business. Maybe it'll be people who want the opposite.

Any group, any organized few, can do it. Not every group will. Most won't. It takes luck, including the luck of good leadership. It takes an environment ripe for change. Mainly, it takes the effective execution of all the strategies we've examined. But as Prohibition teaches us, perhaps not every group that *can* do it—perform power in a self-fulfilling and transformative way—*should*.

Which brings us to the question of ends and moral purposes. Why does a group want to get and wield power? Why does *your* group? Why do *you*?

That's the question for the next and final part of the book.

PART IV

THE WHY OF POWER

THE THREE I'S: INTEGRITY, INCLUSION, INTEREST

Let's end with the beginning in mind.

Power, as I defined it at the outset, is the capacity to ensure that others do as you would like them to do. It takes many forms and flows through many conduits. There are three fundamental laws of how power works, and those laws yield three fundamental imperatives for you the citizen:

- Power creates monopolies, and is winner-take-all → You must change the *game*.
- Power creates a story of why it's legitimate → You must change the *story*.
- Power is assumed to be finite and zero-sum → You must change the *equation*.

Each of these imperatives, in turn, entails certain strategies for action. We've just done a deep dive into those strategies for changing the game, the story, and the equation of power wherever you are. We've looked at the *what* of civic power and the *how*. Now comes the part only you can answer: *Why?*

To what end do you want to become more literate in power? For whose benefit?

Power, remember, is like fire. It is inherently neither good nor evil. It can be put to all kinds of uses. What determines how power is deployed is you: your character, your ethics, your motives. This, indeed, is yet another way that you're more powerful than you think. You, at every turn, are the one in charge of determining why you want power, and why you give it or use it the way you do.

But in this era of concentrated wealth, severe inequality, and rigged rules we have a master narrative that power *is* inherently evil. That's why the civic myths of this age are dark political melodramas like *House of Cards* and grim fantasies like *Game of Thrones* in which nice guys finish headless and the only winners are those who lie, cheat, and kill. We're not in *The West Wing* anymore, folks. Mr. Smith died in Washington.

These times can make it seem like childish thinking to believe you can make a difference or move the system. They make it seem savvy to believe in conspiracy and futility: to adopt the cynic's worldview. And this is deadly. For all the anger in our political culture today, it is not rage that most threatens the legitimacy of our democracy. Rage is healthy even when it is ugly. It forces reckoning. You can respond to rage, whether it comes from the left or right or the disenfranchised unaligned, with a call to action: *Don't get mad; get power.*

What's far more threatening than rage is cynicism. Cynicism is self-confirming and self-fulfilling. Distrust of others and of our institutions spreads rapidly because it gives other people—gives you—permission to be *unworthy* of trust. Cynicism denies the possibility of remedy or the need for responsibility. Worst of all, it blinds us to this central truth:

We can evolve. We have evolved. We are still evolving.

Humans have been able with each succeeding eon to see more of the big picture of our interdependence and to appreciate the gains to our well-being made possible by that interdependence. Over time, more societies have come to realize that cooperation is as useful as competition, "power with" as necessary for a sustainable society as "power over," and freedom something greater than the mere removal of constraints.

In his deeply wise book, *Bonds That Make Us Free*, the educator C. Terry Warner describes a universal human dynamic of "collusion," in which we *accuse* others in order to *excuse* ourselves—and they return the favor. It starts with

A: Why didn't you take out the trash?
B: Well, why didn't you do the dishes?

And it goes to

A: Why don't you fund failing schools?
B: Well, why don't you fire failing teachers?

Or to

A: Why can't black lives matter?

B: Well, why can't blue lives matter?

We accuse to excuse, incessantly, in private and public life alike. But Warner shows us that we can reset this loop. We can convert it from a vicious circle of *denying* responsibility into a virtuous cycle of *accepting* it. When we admit our part of the problem, we free ourselves from the burdens of constant self-serving justification. We influence others by letting them influence us, which awakens *their* sense of responsibility. We create a power that is not contrary to compassion and cooperation but *is* compassion and cooperation.

As a counselor and teacher, Warner has helped people at every scale apply these insights, from families in crisis to corporations in transition to nations at war. Every scale holds the same truth: We make one another. For better or for worse.

Power, then, is an expression of our moral mindset. Of our moral *purpose*. And every power structure is the residue of a set of moral choices. The set of choices called "every man for himself" or "it's not my problem" generates one kind of society; the one called "we're all better off when we're all better off" another.

So as you try to define your own *why* of power, reflect on these three questions:

- Do you integrate character and power?
- Do you try to ensure that more people can participate in power?
- Do you define your self-interest as mutual interest?

These are questions about *integrity*, *inclusion*, and *interest*. The Three I's. Let's unpack each one.

INTEGRITY

Ethics without power is philosophy. Power without ethics is sociopathy. The effective citizen practices both ethics and power. The effective citizen has integrity, in this sense of *integration*, of a wholeness greater than the parts.

Do you integrate character and power?

When I say "character," I don't mean individual virtues like diligence or perseverance or punctuality or moderation. Those are important, of course. But I mean *character in the collective*: social virtues such as generosity, compassion, service, civility, courtesy, and what David Hume and other thinkers of the Scottish Enlightenment called benevolence.

Benevolence is more than mere kind-heartedness and less than pure altruism. It is being actively concerned about the fortune of others because the fortune of others signals something about the environment that will shape our own fortunes. Fundamentally, it means wanting to be *useful* to others.

So when Teddy Roosevelt railed against "*malefactors* of great wealth" at the peak of the last Gilded Age, he was not just using a fancy word for villains; he was berating *non-benefactors*, people without benevolence or a spirit of reciprocity or an awareness of interrelatedness—people who were sociopathic in their pursuit of wealth and willing to tip over the whole economy for their own gain.

Power, when coupled with character in the collective, makes for meaningful citizenship. Knowing how to get what you want *and* caring about what others want is a combination that makes a person and a community prosper in every way.

But it's not easy. Alexis de Tocqueville warned that as the economy and government of America got bigger, citizens could become smaller: less practiced in the forms of everyday power, more dependent on vast distant social machines, more isolated and atomized—and therefore more susceptible to despotism.

He warned that if the "habits of the heart" fed by civic clubs and active self-government evaporated, citizens would regress to pure egoism. They would stop thinking about things greater than their immediate circle. Public life would disappear. And that would only accelerate their own disempowerment.

This is painfully close to a description of the United States since Trump and Europe since Brexit. And the only way to reverse this vicious cycle of retreat and atrophy is to reverse it: to find a sense of purpose that is greater than the self, and to exercise power with others and for others in democratic life. To rediscover those habits of the heart, however, we have to cultivate a habit that precedes all this: being honest, especially with ourselves.

This sense of integrity calls to mind not the great philosophers but the popular ABC television show *What Would You Do?* Each week, the show creates hidden-camera scenarios in which actors stage moral dilemmas that bystanders and passersby respond to (or fail to). You're sitting at a restaurant and you overhear two parents berating their son when he tells them he's gay. You're in line at the toy store and the woman ahead of you realizes she can't afford the gift she promised her son. A young black man comes into a high-end jewelry store and the sales staff follows him closely, loudly insinuating that the only reason he's there is to steal. *What would you do?*

Every one of these scenarios has broader, more systemic civic counterparts. You're on the bus and you hear someone behind you spitting insults at another passenger who's wearing a *hijab*. You're running errands downtown and you stumble upon a march that's just forming to protest a police killing in your community. You're at an office party and meet someone's spouse, a veteran just back from Afghanistan who isn't getting the health care he needs.

What would you do? What *will* you do when you find yourself in such a situation, as you surely will? Be honest. Will you make up a story about how undeserving the person is so that you don't have to help him or her? Will you say to yourself that it isn't your problem? Will you convince yourself that even though you care, you don't have enough power to do anything about the issue anyway?

Or will you instead decide to make yourself useful? Will you choose to learn more, do more, engage more? We are surrounded continuously by the power that we and others generate. We are surrounded continuously by moral choices. Choose integrity.

INCLUSION

This brings us to the second question: Do you try to ensure that more people can participate in power?

Recall the framework about monopoly from the start of the book. Economies and polities are not static machines. They are complex adaptive systems, like natural ecosystems, that naturally create monopolies. As resources concentrate into fewer hands, a contagion of hoarding takes hold until eventually circulation stops and people panic. Picture a bank run, of the kind that happens in *It's a Wonderful Life*. That is happening in slow-motion in America today, with *social* capital as well as financial.

Which is why the citizens and institutions of a healthy society have to be obsessed with busting "opportunity monopolies" and recycling the unearned privilege that comes with them. This means a program of *relentless* inclusion, so that more people are always getting more of a chance to apply their talents and to challenge entrenched rentiers.

Societies that figure out how to sustain inclusion outperform and outlast those that do not. That is the lesson of human history. A century ago, the jurist Louis Brandeis laid out a politics to unclot monopolies and break up unhealthy bigness both in the market and in government. What would a Brandeisian agenda for our own times look like?

There are elements today's left would like: A much more robust inheritance tax. A progressive revenue source for public schools delinked from property values. Higher wages for the working poor, and easier ways for workers to organize and bargain. Democracy vouchers and other public campaign-finance experiments to give everyday voters more power to be donors. Capital requirements and a "size tax" for financial institutions. Antitrust enforcement that keeps firms from becoming abusive monopolists.

There are also elements the right would favor: Unwinding corporate subsidies and cronyism on Wall Street and in government contracting. A radical simplification of the tax code so that tax breaks evaporate and no longer flow overwhelmingly to affluent families. Changes to union rules that make it easier to replace poor performers. Limits on the scale of government agencies so that they don't become "too big to succeed."

Then there are elements that could scramble ideological expectations: Killing the alumni preference in college admissions and creating a poverty preference. A guaranteed basic income. Baby bonuses. A draft—for women and men alike, either for armed or civilian service. An expansion of jury duty to other forms of participation—on local commissions, say. A longer freeze of the revolving door from government to the private sector. A radical push of responsibility—with real funding attached—to what Brandeis called "laboratories of democracy" in states and cities.

Every public policy should be put to a simple test in a politics against monopoly: Does it enable insiders to corner the market on opportunity and voice? Does it reward the already privileged and entrenched for being privileged and entrenched? If so, unwind it.

But put aside policy. Every act of power in your own civic life, individual or collective, should be put to a similar test: Are your actions meant to get more people onto the economic and political playing field? Or to protect those who today dominate the game?

Face your privilege. Privilege is the unearned advantage you get from a past allocation of power. Everyone has some form of privilege. You may not *feel* it or want to admit it. You may have way less of it than the people you are eyeing resentfully or enviously. But when you take an honest accounting of what was conferred upon you at birth by gender or color or class or place or beauty or body, it is impossible to end up with a blank ledger.

You've got something. Then comes a binary choice: to hoard or to circulate.

Why, you might ask, should I circulate and share? Why include more people in the game or give up any of my scarce social, political, and economic capital? Why should I be the sucker who surrenders my edge? How is that possibly in my interest?

The answer—from science, from history, from religion—is that hoarding will hurt you and circulating will help you. And to see that, it helps to have a new mindset about what your *interest* is. Which takes us to the third question.

INTEREST

Do you define your self-interest as mutual interest?

Remember: *power is positive-sum*. It is not zero-sum. When we imagine it to be zero-sum—as Southern whites did when the once-enslaved became citizens—we act in ways that are paranoid and self-subverting. We drive ourselves insane. We create the very scarcity that we fear.

When we imagine power to be positive-sum, we make abundance possible.

In a physical system, energy cannot be created or destroyed. Each gain must come with an equal loss. But in an ecosystem of *relationships*, there is no inherent limit on the aggregate amount of power. Your gain does not have to be my loss. Your gain can be mine as well. After Jackie Robinson integrated baseball, he made every white ballplayer better off because they were now all participants in a game that had more legitimacy, more fans, and more revenue than before.

Self-interest is constant. How we *define* self-interest is changeable. It is, in fact, constantly changing. In recent decades, as American culture has become more market-minded and coarsely materialistic, our ideas about self-interest have grown ever more pinched and zero-sum and hyper-individualistic.

But a different story is emerging. Thanks in part to the burgeoning new science of complex, interdependent systems, it is possible now to see that true self-interest, *properly understood*, is mutual. We are simply too connected for it to be otherwise. There is no way to wall off my fate from yours, my plenty from your lack, or my power from your powerlessness.

If you understand that climate change, obesity, opioid use, gun violence, religious extremism, political corruption, teen pregnancy, and so many other pathologies are contagious, networked phenomena, then you must conclude that there really is no such thing as someone else's problem. You also see that win-wins are what life's winners seek. If you want to thrive, you make sure those around you are thriving.

To be sure, some conflicts are quite zero-sum and others are positive-sum only "in the long run," when, as Keynes famously quipped, we are all dead. And to say that true self-interest is mutual interest is not to say we should pretend we have no interests at all. The Federalist framers of the Constitution sometimes imagined that they, and the system they designed, could manage the grubby competition of interests by rising above it all. Disinterested gentlemen would reign.

The *Anti*-Federalists like Thomas Paine scoffed at this, saying that "disinterested gentlemen" were just another elite with their own particular wants, needs, and preferences. Disinterestedness was a myth, they said, a false front.

They were largely right. Citizens are never without private interests. Wealthy slave-owning planters from Virginia such as Thomas Jefferson were decidedly members of a particular interest group. It was an aristocratic interest, with great power, and one measure of that power was how its members could paint themselves as disinterested.

But the Anti-Federalists were wrong, or at least failed to see the whole picture, when they claimed that citizens are capable of pursuing *only* their private interests, narrowly defined. It is possible—in fact vital—for citizens to pursue their self-interest while also realizing that true self-interest is mutual. Jefferson, parochial Southerner and cosmopolitan American patriot, was actually proof of that.

So here's the test for you, as a practitioner of power: Do you define your interest in ways that are more than purely self-centered? If so, is it because you wish to *appear* disinterested? Or because you truly get that we're all better off when we're all better off?

It takes an act of moral imagination to see that. But if you practice power *without* seeing it, you will be limiting the range of change you can create. You will, in short, be less powerful than you could have been.

THE CONTESTS AHEAD

Of course, there is nothing magical about these three I's. In the hands of an expert rationalizer—which is to say, any of us—all three questions about integrity, inclusion, and interest can be answered in self-justifying, shortsighted ways.

Moreover, power in a democracy always involves contests between not just material interests but moral preferences. Your love of liberty will eventually come into tension with my love of equality. You can resolve that conflict by saying that there is no meaningful liberty without a prior baseline of civic equality, as Danielle Allen does in her beautifully argued book, *Our Declaration*. But someone else can resolve it by saying that meaningful equality cannot exist without real liberty first—in short, the exact opposite.

So there is no final, correct answer to the question *Why exercise power?* In the American political context, the best we can hope for is perpetual contest. America doesn't just have arguments; America *is* an argument: between Federalist and Anti-Federalist worldviews, strong national government and states' rights, liberty and equality, individual rights and collective responsibility, color-blindness and color-consciousness, *Pluribus* and *Unum*.

This is perhaps our highest shared value as Americans: to argue over our values. If we are lucky, these arguments will never end, because if they've ended it means one side will have collapsed, which means eventually the American experiment will as well.

But as we engage in these arguments about how to allocate resources and prioritize our ideals, we can at least learn to have *better* arguments—ones informed by a sense of wisdom that extends the horizon of our intentions and our understanding of consequences. That is the point of asking the three questions about integrity, inclusion, and interest: to push along our evolution as citizens and as a society.

It's high time for such an evolution.

Think about the United States in 1830, when every stream of individual activity eventually fed into the institution of slavery and what its critics called the Slave Power. Slavery—whether in the fields of the South or the ledger books of the North—was as seemingly unmovable as the Mississippi River. But by 1840, enough free people had begun to ask why this should be so, and a movement to confront the enslavers had arisen. By 1850, the sense of imminent crisis was undeniable. By 1860, the conflict had arrived, changing the course of human events.

My point isn't that the United States today is approaching another Civil War. It's that the Civil War started long before 1860. In those decades of rising tension and grim, implacable polarization, some citizens felt the changes coming. Some sped the changes along. Some denied or resisted them.

What would you have done?

What would a *citizen* do? For the most part in this book I have not spoken of leaders and leadership. I have spoken of citizens and citizenship. Being a citizen is not just a matter of literacy in power. It is a matter of coupling that literacy with moral purpose. When you do that, you can challenge any of the givens of a given array of wealth, access, and advantage. You can start the new cascades of belief and behavior that our "leaders" will eventually, even if reluctantly, join. You can write future history.

This kind of citizenship is hard.

Indeed, many Americans would rather not have to do that much work. In his classic, *The True Believer*, Eric Hoffer examined the psychology of mass movements and described how in times of great turbulence, what many seek is not freedom but "freedom from freedom." They want someone else to be responsible, both in the sense of "at fault" and in the sense of "accountable." They become entranced by strongmen who will wield power in our name.

Hoffer wrote in the wake of Nazism and fascism and in the midst of the Cold War. But he describes a strong current of our own times and the culture of Trumpism.

Our choice is not about the presidency or any election. It is about whether we as free people respond to a sense of powerlessness by claiming our full actual power—or by surrendering it altogether. "Strong people don't need strong leaders," the civil rights activist Ella Baker once said.

Are we strong people?

We in the United States have an opportunity now to create the planet's first mass multicultural democratic republic. Ancient Athens was a democracy but not mass, multicultural, or a republic. Rome's republic was multicultural and democratic but not mass. The Soviet Union was mass, multicultural, and a republic but not democratic.

No nation has ever hit all four marks. Including the United States. And it is unclear whether the United States will. What is certain is that we are at the birthing of a new America: the beautiful, painful, bloody arrival of a new majority that does not call itself white. This new America is arriving at precisely the same time when our national government is locked in sclerosis, our economy is warped to send prosperity to the already prosperous, and our sense of shared memory and common culture is dissipating. That all these circumstances are converging now guarantees nothing except contest and conflict.

So then:

Do you *dare* integrate character and power?

Do you *dare* work to ensure that more people can participate in power?

Do you *dare* define self-interest as mutual interest?

Only you know your most candid answers to these questions. Together, they form an atlas for your own quest for purpose. *Who are you—and who are you for?* Together, they remind us that it takes courage to live like a citizen.

EPILOGUE
THEY/WE

I recently caught myself, over the course of a day, saying "they" many times.

> *They decided school will now start an hour later, even though that screws up everyone's commute.*
>
> *They made it hard to opt out of the more expensive insurance plan.*
>
> *When are they going to clean up these abandoned lots?*
>
> *I hate the way they just ignore reality and live in their partisan bubble.*
>
> *They have been swooping in and changing the entire character of the community.*

After I caught myself, I decided in each case to replace "they" with "we."

We decided school would start later. *We* made it hard to opt out. When are *we* going to clean up? I hate the way *we* just ignore reality. *We* are changing the character of the community.

You, too, can perform this find-and-replace function. It's easy to execute. It's more difficult to accept. It forces us to admit that we are always the co-creators of the situations we don't like. (Let's own that.) It reveals how often and how casually we otherize others. (Let's stop that.) And it reminds us that we are always someone else's they. (Let's catch ourselves.)

We can make a bigger we. Starting now. That's where all power begins.

ACKNOWLEDGMENTS

Rafe Sagalyn has been my literary agent for a quarter century, and for that I am so grateful. He's been my champion, counselor, and friend. And he saw the potential for this book even before I did. His colleagues at ICM/Sagalyn, Brandon Coward and Abby Serino, are a delight to work with as well. I'm also thankful for Ben Adams, my editor at PublicAffairs, who combines a command of structure and strategy with a subtle eye for detail. He pushed me to make this book as good as it could be, and I loved his edits. This is the second time I've gotten to work with Ben and the entire first-rate PublicAffairs team: Sandra Beris, Pete Garceau, Jaime Leifer, Josephine Moore, Peter Osnos, Clive Priddle, and Michele Wynn. I'm proud to be published by PublicAffairs.

This book was the direct result of a TED Talk I gave on citizen power, and I want to acknowledge Chris Anderson and his savvy team at TED and TED-Ed and especially my friends Courtney Martin and John Cary, who first brought me into the fold at TED.

In a deeper sense, this book emerges out of the work of Citizen University and at the Aspen Institute Citizenship & American Identity Program. My teammates are extraordinary in their talent, passion, and creativity: Jená Cane, Arista Burwell-Chen, and Ben Phillips at Citizen University, and Carrie Hopper at Aspen. I am so lucky we get to play together through such purposeful work. I also want to thank all the catalytic leaders and activists whose work I describe in these pages, many of whom are members of the Civic Collaboratory, the national network that Citizen University convenes. And I'm grateful to leaders at the Aspen Institute, particularly Kitty Boone, Elliot Gerson, Melissa Ingber, and Walter Isaacson, who've inspired me and given me space to develop my ideas.

Several bright and dedicated young people did research that informed and shaped every part of this book, and I'm in their debt: Hannah Duncan, Jake Levin, and Hasher Nisar came to Citizen University through the Harry S. Truman Foundation, and Trey Leigh and Erwin Li through Yale College. They all will be shaping our country in the years ahead.

I am also deeply grateful to the generous friends who read and critiqued drafts of the manuscript and talked with me about its underlying ideas: Yoni Appelbaum, Bill Budinger, Arista Burwell-Chen, Nick Hanauer, Courtney Martin, Ben Phillips, and Rob Stein. Scott Stossel at *The Atlantic*, Yoni Appelbaum at TheAtlantic.com, Michael Tomasky at *Democracy*, and Rich Galant at CNN.com also influenced this book by inviting me to write essays for them on various aspects of power.

I thank my mother, Julia Liu, for always giving me perceptive, unvarnished feedback on my ideas and how to communicate them. She has a great instinct for American public sentiment. And most of all, I thank my wife, Jená Cane, and my daughter, Olivia Liu, for putting up with the long months of writing when I was chained to the chair and laptop and, more fundamentally, for being joyful and playful even in serious times. Jená, as always, was my first, most trusted reader. She is my partner in this work of reimagining citizenship and in the bigger project of making a beautiful life.

FURTHER READING

Following is a selection of some of the most provocative, interesting books that have shaped my thinking on power. This is not a comprehensive bibliography on the subject, but I hope you'll find it useful. Another source of inspiration, of course, was each day's news. Some outlets, for example, *The New York Times*, have done deep dives on systemic forms of game rigging such as the overuse of arbitration. Other outlets, whether daily newspapers or political magazines from the left or the right, offer an abundance of dispatches about citizen power in action, including the stories documented in this book. Others still, including academic journals, describe some of the theories of power that I refer to throughout.

BOOKS

Acemoglu, Daron, and James A. Robinson. *Why Nations Fail: The Origins of Power, Prosperity, and Poverty*. New York: Crown Business, 2012.
Alinsky, Saul D. *Reveille for Radicals*. New York: Vintage, 1969.
———. *Rules for Radicals: A Pragmatic Primer for Realistic Radicals*. New York: Vintage, 1971.

Allen, Danielle. *Our Declaration: A Reading of the Declaration of Independence in Defense of Equality*. New York: Liveright, 2014.

Arendt, Hannah. *On Revolution*. New York: Penguin, 2006.

Bayat, Asef. *Life as Politics: How Ordinary People Change the Middle East*. Stanford, CA: Stanford University Press, 2010.

Branch, Taylor. *Parting the Waters: America in the King Years 1954–63*. New York: Simon and Schuster, 1988.

Canetti, Elias. *Crowds and Power*. New York: Farrar, Straus and Giroux, 1984.

Carmichael, Stokely, and Charles V. Hamilton. *Black Power: The Politics of Liberation*. New York: Vintage, 1967.

Caro, Robert A. *The Power Broker: Robert Moses and the Fall of New York*. New York: Vintage, 1975.

————. *The Years of Lyndon Johnson: The Path to Power*. New York: Vintage, 1981.

Crouch, Andy. *Playing God: Redeeming the Gift of Power*. Downers Grove, IL: InterVarsity Press, 2013.

Dahl, Robert A. *Who Governs: Democracy and Power in an American City*. New Haven, CT: Yale University Press, 1974.

de Tocqueville, Alexis. *Democracy in America*. New York: Harper and Row, 1966.

Frank, Barney. *Frank: A Life in Politics from the Great Society to Same-Sex Marriage*. New York: Farrar, Straus and Giroux, 2015.

Freedman, Lawrence. *Strategy: A History*. Oxford: Oxford University Press, 2011.

Fukuyama, Francis. *The Origins of Political Order: From Prehuman Times to the French Revolution*. New York: Farrar, Straus and Giroux, 2011.

————. *Political Order and Political Decay: From the Industrial Revolution to the Globalization of Democracy*. New York: Farrar, Straus and Giroux, 2014.

Graeber, David. *The Utopia of Rules: On Technology, Stupidity, and the Secret Joys of Bureaucracy*. New York: Melville House, 2015.

Grewal, David Singh. *Network Power: The Social Dynamics of Globalization*. New Haven, CT: Yale University Press, 2008.

Hamilton, Alexander, James Madison, and John Jay. *The Federalist Papers*. Edited by Clinton Rossiter. New York: Signet, 2003.

Havel, Václav. *Summer Meditations*. New York: Vintage, 1993.

Hayek, F. A. *The Road to Serfdom*. Edited by Bruce Caldwell. Chicago: Chicago University Press, 2007.

Hoffer, Eric. *The True Believer: Thoughts on the Nature of Mass Movements*. New York: Harper Perennial, 1951.

Howard, Philip K. *The Rule of Nobody: Saving America from Dead Laws and Broken Government*. New York: W. W. Norton, 2014.

Hyde, Lewis. *The Gift: Creativity and the Artist in the Modern World*. New York: Vintage, 2007.

Isaacson, Walter. *Benjamin Franklin: An American Life*. New York: Simon and Schuster, 2003.

Keltner, Dachner. *The Power Paradox: How We Gain and Lose Influence*. New York: Penguin, 2016.

Ketcham, Ralph, ed. *The Anti-Federalist Papers*, various authors. New York: Signet, 1986.

Lappé, Frances Moore. *Getting a Grip 2: Clarity, Creativity and Courage for the World We Really Want*. Cambridge, MA: Small Planet Media, 2007.

Lee-Choi, Annette Y., and John Bargh, eds. *The Use and Abuse of Power: Multiple Perspectives on the Causes of Corruption*. New York: Psychology Press, 2001.

Levin, Yuval. *The Fractured Republic: Renewing America's Social Contract in the Age of Individualism*. New York: Basic Books, 2016.

Liu, Eric, and Nick Hanauer. *The Gardens of Democracy: A New American Story of the Economy, Citizenship, and the Role of Government*. Seattle: Sasquatch, 2011.

Lukes, Steven. *Power: A Radical View*. London: Palgrave Macmillan, 2005.

Mandela, Nelson. *Long Walk to Freedom: The Autobiography of Nelson Mandela*. New York: Back Bay Books, 1995.

Mann, Michael. *The Sources of Social Power. Volume 1: A History of Power from the Beginning to AD 1760*. Cambridge: Cambridge University Press, 1986.

Mills, C. Wright. *The Power Elite*. Oxford: Oxford University Press, 1956.

Moynihan, Daniel P. *Maximum Feasible Misunderstanding: Community Action in the War on Poverty*. New York: Free Press, 1969.

Murray, Charles. *By the People: Rebuilding Liberty Without Permission*. New York: Crown Forum, 2015.

Naím, Moisés. *The End of Power: From Boardrooms to Battlefields and Churches to States: Why Being in Charge Isn't What It Used to Be*. New York: Basic Books, 2013.

Okrent, Daniel. *Last Call: The Rise and Fall of Prohibition.* New York: Scribner, 2010.

Olson, Mancur. *The Logic of Collective Action: Public Goods and the Theory of Groups.* Cambridge, MA: Harvard University Press, 1965.

Ostrom, Elinor. *Governing the Commons: The Evolution of Institutions for Collective Action.* Cambridge: Cambridge University Press, 1990.

Palmer, Parker. *Healing the Heart of Democracy: The Courage to Create a Politics Worthy of the Human Spirit.* San Francisco: Jossey-Bass, 2011.

Pocock, J. G. A. *Politics, Language and Time: Essays on Political Thought and History.* Chicago: University of Chicago Press, 1989.

Ramo, Joshua Cooper. *The Seventh Sense: Power, Fortune, and Survival in the Age of Networks.* New York: Little, Brown, 2016.

Rolf, David. *The Fight for Fifteen: The Right Wage for a Working America.* New York: The New Press, 2016.

Schattschneider, E. E. *The Semisovereign People: A Realist's View of Democracy in America.* New York: Harcourt, Brace, 1975.

Scott, James C. *Weapons of the Weak: Everyday Forms of Peasant Resistance.* New Haven, CT: Yale University Press, 1985.

———. *Seeing Like a State: How Certain Schemes to Improve the Human Condition Have Failed.* New Haven, CT: Yale University Press, 1998.

Sharp, Gene. *Power and Struggle: Politics of Nonviolent Action (Part 1).* Manchester, NH: Porter Sargent, 1973.

Smith, Adam. *The Theory of Moral Sentiments.* New York: Penguin, 2009.

Solnit, Rebecca. *A Paradise Built in Hell: The Extraordinary Communities That Arise in Disaster.* New York: Penguin, 2009.

Steinem, Gloria. *My Life on the Road.* New York: Random House, 2015.

Stern, Andy, and Lee Kravitz. *Raising the Floor: How a Universal Basic Income Can Renew Our Economy and Rebuild the American Dream.* New York: PublicAffairs, 2016.

Sun Tzu. *The Art of War.* Translated by Samuel B. Griffith. Oxford: Oxford University Press, 1963.

United States Marine Corps. *Warfighting.* Washington, DC: U.S. Government Printing Office, 1989.

Urofsky, Melvin I. *Louis D. Brandeis: A Life.* New York: Schocken, 2009.

van Gelder, Sarah. *The Revolution Where You Live: Stories from a 12,000-Mile Journey Through a New America.* Oakland, CA: Berrett-Koehler, 2017.

Warner, C. Terry. *Bonds That Make Us Free: Healing Our Relationships, Coming to Ourselves.* Salt Lake City, UT: Shadow Mountain, 2001.

Wood, Gordon S. *The Radicalism of the American Revolution*. New York: Vintage, 1991.

OTHER SOURCES

PROLOGUE: IMMOKALEE AND POTTERSVILLE

"About CIW." Coalition of Immokalee Workers. www.ciw-online.org /about.

OUR MOMENT, OUR POWER, OUR PLAN

Gilens, Martin, and Benjamin I. Page. "Testing Theories of American Politics: Elites, Interest Groups, and Average Citizens." *Perspectives on Politics* 12, no. 3 (September 2014): 564–581. doi:10.1017 /S1537592714001595.

THE THREE LAWS OF POWER

The Chicago Community Trust Staff. "How a Glenview Retiree Defeated Unjust Housing Laws." The Chicago Community Trust, December 16, 2015. www.cct.org/2015/12/how-a-glenview-retiree -defeated-unjust-housing-law.

Choi, Juliet, Avani Bhatt, and Frankie Chen. "In the Aftermath of Hurricane Katrina: The Chef Menteur Landfill and Its Effects on the Vietnamese American Community." Washington, DC: Asian American Justice Center, August 2006.

Eaton, Leslie. "A New Landfill in New Orleans Sets Off a Battle." *New York Times*, May 8, 2006. www.nytimes.com/2006/05/08/us /08landfill.html.

Fast, Nathanael J., Nir Halevy, and Adam D. Galinsky. "The Destructive Nature of Power Without Status." *Journal of Experimental Social Psychology* 48, no. 1 (January 2012): 391–394. doi:10.1016/j .jesp.2011.07.013.

Kuosa, Tuomo. "A Few Extensions to Path-Dependence and Emergence in Complex Social Systems." *Emergence: Complexity and Organization* 9, no. 4 (2007): 3–16.

Rios, Kimberly, Nathanael J. Fast, and Deborah H. Gruenfeld. "Feeling High but Playing Low Power, Need to Belong, and Submissive Behavior." *Personality and Social Psychology Bulletin* (June 17, 2015): 0146167215591494. doi:10.1177/0146167215591494.

Sawaoka, Takuya, Brent L. Hughes, and Nalini Ambady. "Power Heightens Sensitivity to Unfairness Against the Self." *Personality and Social Psychology Bulletin* (June 5, 2015): 0146167215588755. doi:10.1177/0146167215588755.

Schilke, Oliver, Martin Reimann, and Karen S. Cook. "Power Decreases Trust in Social Exchange." *Proceedings of the National Academy of Sciences* 112, no. 42 (October 20, 2015): 12950–12955. doi:10.1073 /pnas.1517057112.

Tang, Eric. "A Gulf Unites Us: The Vietnamese Americans of Black New Orleans East." *American Quarterly* 63, no. 1 (2011): 117–149. doi:10.1353/aq.2011.0005.

Turner, Anna. "Determined Mum Establishes Charity." *Stuff*, October 15, 2013, sec. Life & Style. www.stuff.co.nz/life-style/parenting /big-kids/five-to-ten/health-nutrition/9284335/Determined-mum -establishes-charity.

Van der Toorn, Jojanneke, Matthew Feinberg, John T. Jost, Aaron C. Kay, Tom R. Tyler, Robb Willer, and Caroline Wilmuth. "A Sense of Powerlessness Fosters System Justification: Implications for the Legitimation of Authority, Hierarchy, and Government." *Political Psychology* 36, no. 1 (February 1, 2015): 93–110. doi:10.1111/pops.12183.

LEGITIMACY AND THE POWER STRUCTURE

Bergal, Jenni. "A License to Braid Hair? Critics Say State Licensing Rules Have Gone Too Far." Pew Charitable Trusts, Stateline, January 30, 2015. www.pewtrusts.org/en/research-and-analysis/blogs /stateline/2015/1/30/a-license-to-braid-hair-critics-say-state -licensing-rules-have-gone-too-far.

Boudway, Ira, and Kate Smith. "The Braves Play Taxpayers Better than They Play Baseball." Bloomberg, April 27, 2016. www.bloomberg .com/features/2016-atlanta-braves-stadium.

De Rugy, Veronique. "There's At Least One Good Idea in Obama's Budget: Attacking Occupational Licensing." *National Review*, February 2, 2015. www.nationalreview.com /corner/397435/theres-least-one-good-idea-obamas-budget -attacking-occupational-licensing-veronique-de.

Heather, Stephenson, and Kiki Zeldes. "'Write a Chapter and Change the World': How the Boston Women's Health Book Collective Transformed Women's Health Then—and Now." *American Journal of Public Health* 98, no. 10 (October 2008): 1741–1745. doi:10.2105 /AJPH.2007.132159.

Hilsenrath, Jon. "Years of Fed Missteps Fueled Disillusion with the Economy and Washington." *Wall Street Journal*, August 26, 2016, sec. Page One. www.wsj.com/articles/years-of-fed-missteps-fueled -disillusion-with-the-economy-and-washington-1472136026.

Isaac, Mike. "Facebook, Facing Bias Claims, Shows How Editors and Algorithms Guide News." *New York Times*, May 12, 2016. www .nytimes.com/2016/05/13/technology/facebook-guidelines -trending-topics.html.

Powell, Michael. "A School Board That Overlooks Its Obligation to Students." *New York Times*, April 7, 2014. www.nytimes.com /2014/04/08/nyregion/a-school-board-that-overlooks-its-obligation -to-students.html.

"Vindicating Win for Hard-Pressing Advocates Seen in Obama." *MSNBC*, November 19, 2014. www.msnbc.com/rachel-maddow/watch /vindicating-win-seen-by-immigration-advocates-361090627865.

Wotton, Julie. "Despite Opposition, Refugee Services Unlikely to End in Twin Falls." *Twin Falls Times-News*, August 28, 2015. http://magicvalley .com/news/local/despite-opposition-refugee-services-unlikely-to -end-in-twin-falls/article_9b1c7aa2-c1f9-519d-b069-fe1743ed26a2 .html.

CHANGE THE GAME: STRATEGY 1:
ADJUST THE ARENA

"Attorney General Loretta E. Lynch Delivers Remarks at Press Conference Announcing Complaint Against the State of North Carolina to Stop Discrimination Against Transgender Individuals." U.S. Department of Justice, May 9, 2016. www.justice.gov/opa/speech /attorney-general-loretta-e-lynch-delivers-remarks-press -conference-announcing-complaint.

Green, Erica, and Luke Broadwater. "Civil Rights Activist DeRay Mckesson to Join New City Schools Cabinet." *Baltimore Sun*, June 28, 2016. www.baltimoresun.com/news/maryland/baltimore-city/bs-md -ci-deray-mckesson-appointment-20160628-story.html.

Parker, Richard. "How Austin Beat Uber." *New York Times*, May 12, 2016. www.nytimes.com/2016/05/12/opinion/how-austin-beat-uber .html.

Steinmetz, Katy. "Why LGBT Advocates Say Bathroom 'Predators' Are Red Herring." *Time*, May 2, 2016. http://time.com/4314896 /transgender-bathroom-bill-male-predators-argument.

W., A. "Uber and Lyft Have Their Bluff Called in Austin." *The Economist*, May 17, 2016. www.economist.com/blogs/gulliver/2016/05 /game-texas-holdem.

CHANGE THE GAME: STRATEGY 2:
RE-RIG THE RULES

"About KYIX." Know Your IX. http://knowyourix.org/about-ky9.

Bradley, Donald. "KC Man Pays $50,000 Interest on $2,500 in Payday Loans." *Kansas City Star*, May 17, 2016. www.kansascity.com/news /local/article78174997.html.

CCO—Unlocking the Power of People. www.cco.org.

Hall, Terra. "Interfaith Group Calls for 'Moral Economy.'" *KSHB*, September 21, 2015. www.kshb.com/thenow/interfaith-group -calls-for-moral-economy.

Morgenson, Gretchen. "Ending Tax Break for Ultrawealthy May Not Take Act of Congress." *New York Times*, May 6, 2016. www.nytimes .com/2016/05/08/business/ending-tax-break-for-ultrawealthy-may -not-take-act-of-congress.html.

Silver-Greenberg, Jessica, and Michael Corkery. "In Arbitration, a 'Privatization of the Justice System.'" *New York Times*, November 1, 2015. www.nytimes.com/2015/11/02/business/dealbook/in -arbitration-a-privatization-of-the-justice-system.html.

Silver-Greenberg, Jessica, and Robert Gebeloff. "Arbitration Everywhere, Stacking the Deck of Justice." *New York Times*, October 31, 2015. www.nytimes.com/2015/11/01/business/dealbook/arbitration -everywhere-stacking-the-deck-of-justice.html.

Thomson, Janice. "From Curious Citizen to Electric Community— Citizenize-Citizenise." Citizenize-Citizenise. www.janicethomson .net/from-curious-citizen-to-electric-community/.

CHANGE THE GAME: STRATEGY 3:
ATTACK YOUR OPPONENT'S PLAN

Dreier, Peter. "20 Activists Who Are Changing America." *Huffington Post*, November 3, 2013. www.huffingtonpost.com/peter-dreier/activists -changing-america_b_4209480.html.

Moms Demand Action for Gun Sense in America. http://momsdemand action.org.

Sturgis, Sue. "Moral Monday Leader Launches 15-State Tour Calling for More Love in Politics." *Facing South*, March 31, 2016. www.facingsouth .org/2016/03/moral-monday-leader-launches-15-state-tour-calling.

Zimpfer, Travis. "'Medicaid 23' Split Verdict Sparks Anger." *Missouri Times*, August 18, 2016. http://themissouritimes.com/32816 /medicaid-23-split-verdict-sparks-anger.

CHANGE THE STORY: STRATEGY 4: DESCRIBE THE ALTERNATIVE

Choi, Hanna. "Diversity in Hollywood: Here's What Critics Are Saying About Round 2 Of #OscarSoWhite." NPR, January 1, 2016. www .npr.org/sections/codeswitch/2016/01/19/463590839/diversity -in-hollywood-heres-what-critics-are-saying-about-round-2-of -oscarsowhi.

Encore.org—Second Acts for Greater Good. http://encore.org.

Garber, Megan. "Call It the 'Bechdel-Wallace Test.'" *The Atlantic*, August 25, 2015. www.theatlantic.com/entertainment/archive/2015/08 /call-it-the-bechdel-wallace-test/402259.

Mapping Police Violence. http://mappingpoliceviolence.org.

National Domestic Workers Alliance. www.domesticworkers.org.

Poo, Ai-jen. "Why We Need to Support Innovation in Our States— Caring Across Generations." www.caringacross.org/stories/support -innovation-in-our-states.

Steinem, Gloria. "If Men Could Menstruate." http://ww3.haverford.edu /psychology/ddavis/p109g/steinem.menstruate.html.

"Swiss Voters Reject Proposal to Give Basic Income to Every Adult and Child." *The Guardian*, June 5, 2016, sec. World news. www .theguardian.com/world/2016/jun/05/swiss-vote-give-basic-income -every-adult-child-marxist-dream.

"The Problem." Campaign Zero. www.joincampaignzero.org/problem.

CHANGE THE STORY: STRATEGY 5: ORGANIZE IN NARRATIVES

"About." Students for Liberty. http://studentsforliberty.org/about.

Abramsky, Sasha. "A Conversation with Marshall Ganz." *The Nation*, February 3, 2011. www.thenation.com/article/conversation-marshall-ganz.

Bai, Matt. "Wiring the Vast Left-Wing Conspiracy." *New York Times*, July 25, 2004. www.nytimes.com/2004/07/25/magazine/wiring-the -vast-left-wing-conspiracy.html.

Broockman, David, and Joshua Kalla. "Durably Reducing Transphobia: A Field Experiment on Door-to-Door Canvassing." *Science* 352, no. 6282 (April 8, 2016): 220–224. doi:10.1126/science.aad9713.

Define American. https://defineamerican.com.

Foley, Elise. "Jake Brewer's Immigration Legacy May Last for Years." *Huffington Post*, September 21, 2015. www.huffingtonpost.com/entry /jake-brewer-define-american-immigration_us_56003ee8e4b0 fde8b0cf1a54.

The Harry Potter Alliance. www.thehpalliance.org.

Jenkins, Henry. "'Cultural Acupuncture': Fan Activism and the Harry Potter Alliance." *Transformative Works and Cultures* 10 (2012). http:// journal.transformativeworks.org/index.php/twc/article/view/305.

"Powell Memorandum: Attack on American Free Enterprise System." Washington and Lee University School of Law. http://law2.wlu .edu/powellarchives/page.asp?pageid=1251.

Vargas, Jose Antonio. "My Life as an Undocumented Immigrant." *New York Times Magazine*, June 22, 2011. www.nytimes.com/2011/06/26 /magazine/my-life-as-an-undocumented-immigrant.html.

CHANGE THE STORY: STRATEGY 6:
MAKE YOUR FIGHT A FABLE

Aleaziz, Hamed, and Wendy Lee. "Frisco Five Say Hunger Strike Is Over." *SFGate*, May 8, 2016. www.sfgate.com/bayarea/article /Raucous-City-Hall-protest-brings-arrests-7420771.php.

Blackmon, Douglas A., Jennifer Levitz, Alexandra Berzon, and Lauren Etter. "Birth of a Movement." *Wall Street Journal*, October 29, 2010, sec. US. www.wsj.com/articles/SB10001424052702304173704575578 332725182228.

Convention of States. www.conventionofstates.com.

Dokoupil, Tony. "Big Oil Joins Legal Fight Against Little Kids over Climate Change." *MSNBC*, November 12, 2015. www.msnbc.com /msnbc/big-oil-joins-legal-fight-little-kids-over-climate-change.

Ford, Matt. "A Governor Ordered to Serve as a Public Defender." *The Atlantic*, August 4, 2016. www.theatlantic.com/politics /archive/2016/08/when-the-governor-is-your-lawyer/494453.

Fossil Free. http://gofossilfree.org.

Green, Emily, Bob Egelko, Jenna Lyons, and Erin Allday. "SFPD Chief Greg Suhr Resigns After Police Killing of Woman." *SFGate*, May 20, 2016. www.sfgate.com/bayarea/article/Police-Chief-Greg-Suhr -resigns-after-killing-of-7758122.php.

Green, Marcus Harrison. "Anti-Racist Organizers Win as Seattle Council Votes to End Youth Incarceration." *YES! Magazine*, September 22, 2015. www.yesmagazine.org/seattle-organizers-win-city-council -votes-end-youth-incarceration-20150922.

Henn, Jamie, and Clemence Dubois. "Divestment Commitments Pass the $3.4 Trillion Mark at COP21." 350.org, December 2, 2015. https://350.org/press-release/divestment-commitments -pass-the-3–4-trillion-mark-at-cop21.

Krontiris, Kate, John Webb, Chris Chapman, and Charlotte Krontiris. "Understanding America's 'Interested Bystander:' A Complicated Relationship with Civic Duty." *Politics & Elections Blog*, June 3, 2015. https://politics.googleblog.com/2015/06/understanding-americas -interested.html.

McKibben, Bill. "Embarrassing Photos of Me, Thanks to My Right-Wing Stalkers." *New York Times*, August 5, 2016. www.nytimes .com/2016/08/07/opinion/sunday/embarrassing-photos-of-me -thanks-to-my-right-wing-stalkers.html.

"Meet the Youth Plaintiffs." Our Children's Trust. www.ourchildrens trust.org/meet-the-youth-plaintiffs.

Oppel Jr., Richard. "In Tribute to Son, Khizr Khan Offered Citizenship Lesson at Convention." *New York Times*, July 29, 2016. www.nytimes .com/2016/07/29/us/elections/khizr-humayun-khan-speech.html.

Weinstein, Adam. "The Secret History of the Campus Carry Movement." *The Trace*, July 5, 2015. www.thetrace.org/2015/07/the-making -of-the-campus-carry-movement.

CHANGE THE EQUATION: STRATEGY 7: ACT EXPONENTIALLY

"About." Giving Tuesday. www.givingtuesday.org/about.

"Beyond Ferguson." F. Willis Johnson. http://holddownyourcorner .com.

The Center for Social Empowerment. www.thecenterforsocialempower ment.com.

Heimans, Jeremy, and Henry Timms. "Understanding 'New Power.'" *Harvard Business Review*, December 1, 2014. https://hbr.org/2014/12 /understanding-new-power.

Whitford, Emma. "Uber Drivers Can't Unionize, So Some Are Joining 'Self-Help' Association 'Uber ALLES.'" *Gothamist*, April 29, 2016. http://gothamist.com/2016/04/29/1000_nyc_uber_drivers_to _announce_s.php.

CHANGE THE EQUATION: STRATEGY 8:
ACT RECIPROCALLY

Deller, Steven, Ann Hoyt, Brent Hueth, and Reka Sundaram-Stukel. "Research on the Economic Impact of Cooperatives." University of Wisconsin Center for Cooperatives, June 19, 2009. http://reic.uwcc .wisc.edu/sites/all/REIC_FINAL.pdf.

Goodnough, Abby. "Christians Flock to Groups That Help Members Pay Medical Bills." *New York Times*, March 10, 2016. www.nytimes .com/2016/03/11/us/christians-flock-to-groups-that-help-members -pay-medical-bills.html.

"Meet Bob Woodson." Center for Neighborhood Enterprise. www .cneonline.org/woodson-biography.

"The Mikva Model." Mikva Challenge. www.mikvachallenge.org /programs/the-mikva-model.

The Participatory Budgeting Project. www.participatorybudgeting.org.

CHANGE THE EQUATION: STRATEGY 9:
PERFORM POWER

Blumberg, Antonia. "The Gospel According to Bree Newsome." *Huffington Post*, June 30, 2015. www.huffingtonpost.com/2015/06/29 /bree-newsome-faith_n_7692004.html.

"Canceling Cops on Fox." Color of Change. http://colorofchange.org /campaigns/victories/petition_delivery_cops.

Carter, Bill. "ABC Aims for Diversity with Shows Like 'Black-Ish' and 'Fresh Off the Boat.'" *New York Times*, September 3, 2014. www .nytimes.com/2014/09/07/arts/television/abc-aims-for-diversity-with -shows-like-black-ish-and-fresh-off-the-boat.html.

Collins, Scott, and Meredith Blake. "Years Before Court Ruling, Pop Culture Shaped Same-Sex Marriage Debate." *Los Angeles Times*, June 27, 2015. www.latimes.com/entertainment/la-et-st-0628-media -gay-marriage-20150628-story.html.

Creative Exchange. http://springboardexchange.org.

Cuddy, Amy. "Your Body Language Shapes Who You Are." June 2012. TED. www.ted.com/talks/amy_cuddy_your_body_language_shapes _who_you_are?language=en.

Cuddy, Amy J. C. "Want to Lean In? Try a Power Pose." *Harvard Business Review*, March 20, 2013. https://hbr.org/2013/03/want -to-lean-in-try-a-power-po-2.

Genzlinger, Neil. "The Apothetae Aims to Merge Disabilities into the Theatrical Mainstream." *New York Times*, June 29, 2013. www .nytimes.com/2013/06/30/nyregion/the-apothetae-aims-to-merge -disabilities-into-the-theatrical-mainstream.html.

Healy, Jack. "North Dakota Oil Pipeline Battle: Who's Fighting and Why." *New York Times*, August 26, 2016. www.nytimes.com/2016/08/27/us /north-dakota-oil-pipeline-battle-whos-fighting-and-why.html.

Herszenhorn, David M., and Emmarie Huetteman. "House Democrats' Gun-Control Sit-In Turns into Chaotic Showdown with Republi-cans." *New York Times*, June 22, 2016. www.nytimes.com/2016/06/23 /us/politics/house-democrats-stage-sit-in-to-push-for-action-on -gun-control.html.

Hillstrom, Christa. "The Lakota Martial Arts Teacher Helping Native Women Recover Their Strength." *YES! Magazine*, June 28, 2016. www.yesmagazine.org/issues/gender-justice/the-lakota-martial -arts-teacher-helping-native-women-recover-their-strength -20160628.

Pearce, Adam, and Alicia Parlapiano. "Only 9% of America Chose Trump and Clinton as the Nominees." *New York Times*, August 1, 2016. www.nytimes.com/interactive/2016/08/01/us/elections/nine-percent -of-america-selected-trump-and-clinton.html.

Remnick, Noah. "Yale Defies Calls to Rename Calhoun College." *New York Times*, April 27, 2016. www.nytimes.com/2016/04/28/nyregion /yale-defies-calls-to-rename-calhoun-college.html.

Rosenkranz, Nicholas Quinn. "William F. Buckley Program at Yale Hosts Its Second Annual 'Disinvitation Dinner.'" *Washington Post*, May 2, 2016. www.washingtonpost.com/news/volokh-conspiracy/wp /2016/05/02/william-f-buckley-program-at-yale-hosts-its-second -annual-disinvitation-dinner.

Ryan, John. "Hundreds of 'Kayaktivists' in Seattle Protest Shell's Arctic Drilling." NPR, May 18, 2015. www.npr.org/2015/05/18/407619645 /hundreds-of-kayaktivists-in-seattle-protest-shells-arctic-drilling.

Sharp, Gene. *Power and Struggle: Politics of Nonviolent Action (Part I)*. Manchester, NH: Porter Sargent, 1973.

Sidahmed, Mazin. "'She Was Making Her Stand': Image of Baton Rouge Protester an Instant Classic." *The Guardian*, July 11, 2016, sec. US news. www.theguardian.com/us-news/2016/jul/11/baton -rouge-protester-photo-iesha-evans.

"Why Millennials Don't Vote for Mayor: Barriers and Motivators for Local Voting." The Knight Foundation. http://features.knightfoundation .org/local-vote/voter-dropoff.pdf.

Alan Alabastro

Eric Liu is the founder and CEO of Citizen University and executive director of the Aspen Institute Citizenship and American Identity Program. His TED Talks on citizen power and voting have had over 2 million views, and he is the author of several books, including *A Chinaman's Chance* and *The Gardens of Democracy* (coauthored with Nick Hanauer). Liu served as a White House speechwriter and policy adviser for President Bill Clinton. He is a regular columnist for CNN.com and a correspondent for TheAtlantic.com.

PublicAffairs is a publishing house founded in 1997. It is a tribute to the standards, values, and flair of three persons who have served as mentors to countless reporters, writers, editors, and book people of all kinds, including me.

I. F. STONE, proprietor of *I. F. Stone's Weekly*, combined a commitment to the First Amendment with entrepreneurial zeal and reporting skill and became one of the great independent journalists in American history. At the age of eighty, Izzy published *The Trial of Socrates*, which was a national bestseller. He wrote the book after he taught himself ancient Greek.

BENJAMIN C. BRADLEE was for nearly thirty years the charismatic editorial leader of *The Washington Post*. It was Ben who gave the *Post* the range and courage to pursue such historic issues as Watergate. He supported his reporters with a tenacity that made them fearless and it is no accident that so many became authors of influential, best-selling books.

ROBERT L. BERNSTEIN, the chief executive of Random House for more than a quarter century, guided one of the nation's premier publishing houses. Bob was personally responsible for many books of political dissent and argument that challenged tyranny around the globe. He is also the founder and longtime chair of Human Rights Watch, one of the most respected human rights organizations in the world.

.   .   .

For fifty years, the banner of Public Affairs Press was carried by its owner Morris B. Schnapper, who published Gandhi, Nasser, Toynbee, Truman, and about 1,500 other authors. In 1983, Schnapper was described by *The Washington Post* as "a redoubtable gadfly." His legacy will endure in the books to come.

Peter Osnos, *Founder and Editor-at-Large*